Off Grid Living:

The ultimate step-by-step guide to becoming completely self-sufficient

Feed the Knowledge Publishing

Off Grid Living

Copyright © 2022 **Feed The Knowledge Publishing**
All rights reserved.

This document is geared towards providing exact and reliable information in regard to the topic and issue covered.
- From a Declaration of Principles which was accepted and approved equally by a Committee of the American Bar Association and a Committee of Publishers and Associations.
In no way is it legal to reproduce, duplicate, or transmit any part of this document in either electronic means or in printed format. All rights reserved.
The information provided herein is stated to be truthful and consistent, in that any liability, in terms of inattention or otherwise, by any usage or abuse of any policies, processes, or directions contained within is the solitary and utter responsibility of the recipient reader. Under no circumstances will any legal responsibility or blame be held against the publisher for any reparation, damages, or monetary loss due to the information herein, either directly or indirectly.
Respective authors own all copyrights not held by the publisher.
The information herein is offered for informational purposes solely and is universal as so. The presentation of the information is without contract or any type of guarantee assurance.
The trademarks that are used are without any consent, and the publication of the trademark is without permission or backing by the trademark owner. All trademarks and brands within this book are for clarifying purposes only and are owned by the owners themselves, not affiliated with this document.

Off Grid Living

Catalog

Introduction	7
Why Go Off-Grid?	11
Places to Start	19
Water	21
Efforts Made to Save Water	23
Wells	24
Springs	29
Catchment systems allow for the collection of precipitation.	34
Putting Your Water to the Test	38
Water-Source Hygiene	39
Heating systems for the water	40
Heaters that Use Heat Pumps	41
Water heaters that work indirectly	42
Heaters That Are Either On-Demand Or Tankless	42
Solar heaters for the water	44
Getting Started with the Use of Solar Energy to Heat Water	45
The Fundamental Vocabulary Used in Solar Water Heating Systems	46
Solar water heating system components and their functions.	48
Collectors	49

Off Grid Living

Collectors Using Flat Plates (FPCs)	51
Collectors for Evacuated Gases in Tubes (ETCs)	52
Collectors That Focus Their Energy	54
Collectors of the Pools	54
Mounts for Collectors	55
Solar Storage Tanks	56
Water Pump	57
Heat Exchanger	58
Expansion Tanks	59
Differential Controls	60
Isolation Valve (Solar Bypass)	61
Tempering Valve	62
Emergency Water Heater as a Backup	62
Several Distinct Categories of Solar-Powered Water Heaters	63
Batch (ICS) Systems	63
Systems for Thermosiphoning (TS)	64
Open-Loop Direct Systems	65
Systematization of Pressurized Solar Fluid (Glycol)	66
Drainage-Back Systems With a Closed Loop	68
Food	70
Growing Your Garden	75
Conservation of Resources	85
Landscaping	87

Off Grid Living

Home Appliances That Use Less Energy	90
Home Improvements	93
Lighting	95
Heating and Cooling of the Ambient Air	98
Refrigeration	101
Laundry	103
Steaming Water	104
Dishwashing	105
Cooking	106
Transportation	107
Generating Energy	110
Energy through Heat	115
Convection	118
The Astonishing Actuality Concerning Electricity	120
Photovoltaic Cells	125
Wind Systems	141
Sizing Your System	143
Controllers of Electrical Charge	150
Inverters	152
Housing	154
Construction Using Only the Sun's Energy	158
Transient Shelters	167
Tents and other forms of soft shelter	167
The Living Space	172

Off Grid Living

Durability	174
Defense against the effects of water	175
Protection against Insects	177
Yurts	178
Traditional Homes of the Indigenous Peoples of the United States	181
Vehicles for Pleasure or Recreation (RVs)	184
Waste Management	186
Recycling	187
Sewage	189
sewage treatment plants	192
Toilets that Compost Waste	195
Maintaining the Contentment of Your Composter	198
Primitive Methods of Waste Disposal	199
Transient Toilets	201
Latrines	205
Conclusion	208
References:	209

Introduction

Those who are equipped with the necessary level of tenacity, problem-solving abilities, and survival knowledge may convert even a relatively small piece of land into a resource that is perpetually productive thanks to the abundance that the Earth provides. Going off the grid is an enticing concept to many people since it entails living each and every day in the open air and developing a style of life that is more environmentally friendly. By adopting a more natural way of life, you may reduce your impact on the natural world, acquire the skills necessary to become completely independent and take pleasure in the myriad of things that Mother Nature has to offer. But subsisting solely off the land is not for the faint of heart or those who are not well equipped. It takes years of foundation and skill-honing to get to a position where you can exist (and flourish) without

Off Grid Living

the municipal utilities, food shops, and other services that we take for granted every day in our everyday lives.

The notion of living off the grid is an alluring one, isn't it? Imagine being fully independent, in the sense that you produce all of your own electricity, cultivate all of your own food, and raise all of your own animals, and that you are free from the 'connected' systems that civilization provides... It's hard to put yourself in that situation, isn't it? We are very dependent on the fact that power is accessible at the flip of a switch and that we can go to the store whenever we want to get whatever food we want.

Do not be alarmed if the thought of going much farther than that causes you to break out in a cold sweat. In this discussion, we will focus on off-grid living, which refers to a lifestyle in which food can still be purchased, but in which residents are able to live independently from the national power grid by producing their own electricity using the Earth's natural resources, most commonly wind or solar energy.

Put a large number of individuals of varying ages in the same room. Conservatives and liberals both share this view. Rich, middle-class, and impoverished to a shocking degree. The complete spectrum of human life in the United States includes athletes, soldiers, blue-collar and white-collar employees, criminals, and priests. If you were to ask them what the term "off-grid" implies, you would get hundreds of meanings that pertain to people, things, trends, and activities that are not conventional.

Someone who does not make use of social networking sites such as MySpace or Facebook is referred to as an "off-grid" by teenagers.

It might imply that you are unable to be tracked, recognized, or recorded using conventional

Off Grid Living

methods if you are speaking to a private investigator or researcher.

It may involve going underground, avoiding all recordable means of trade, and using only cash in order to steer clear of any transactions that may be traced in the case of a person who is paranoid, antisocial, or a criminal on the run.

It may entail engaging in daring, life-threatening activities in far-flung, unexplored parts of the world for a person who participates in extreme sports.

"Off the grid" is a term that may be used to describe a brilliant but absentminded lecturer to a group of college students studying science.

Off-grid will be defined by me as a state or degree of self-sufficiency with little dependence on public utilities, particularly the three conventional essentials of electricity (power), water, and waste management, for the sake of this discussion. Locations are considered to be "off-grid" when they are completely independent of the services provided by public utilities in the areas of energy production, water management, and waste disposal.

Why Go Off-Grid?

- ➤ There is no grid that may be used at this time. This may be a result of free will or predetermined events. There is a significant population of individuals living in Third World nations and even in rural areas of the United States who do not have access to the typical grid's utilities. It's possible that you're wealthy and has discovered the property of your dreams, but unfortunately, it's located too far out in the country to be connected to the power grid. Or maybe you're dirt poor, and you don't have access to the power grid because you live in the filth of a grid-less mud hamlet in the Andes. It's possible that you live in a religious group that shuns the comforts of contemporary life. The typical grid is not present here for whatever reason it may be.

- "In order to reduce the grid's negative effects on the environment." in order to lessen your "carbon footprint" and help the planet recover from all of the damage that humans have caused to it.
- In order to save money and avoid the exorbitant costs associated with standard utility hookups. This line of thinking is prevalent among affluent people who own numerous residences but only occupy some of them on a temporary basis.
- In order to cut costs and save money on power bills. Under the present conditions, this is nothing more than a pipe dream. It is true that you have to spend money in order to save money, and achieving financial independence requires a significant financial investment. You

Off Grid Living

may be able to get rid of your electricity bills by making a significant investment, but you will still have to pay monthly fees (battery replacement, etc.).

- To guarantee that you continue to have access to services in the event that the grid fails. This is perhaps the most compelling and logical argument in favor of reducing the amount of energy you get from the grid. It's possible that you're a survivalist, but it's also possible that you're simply an ordinary parent trying to make the best possible preparations for your family in the event of an emergency.
- To entertain a clever mind. If you are someone who enjoys tinkering with mechanical and electrical devices and truly enjoys physics, chemistry, and electronics, then this is life for you.
- To lessen our reliance on fossil fuels, particularly oil, as a country. During the years

Off Grid Living

2007 and 2008, we were all appalled to watch as the price of oil pulled our economy into the abyss. During this time, our children were still being killed on the streets of Baghdad as part of a "war on terror" that was more concerned with oil than it was with fighting terrorists. Perhaps there is no more satisfying form of vengeance than financial retribution. Instead of invading hostile governments, we need to put in a lot of effort to be in a position where we can boycott the oil they produce.

- Image in the public eye. This is the very worst justification for living off the grid. Being able to adopt environmentally friendly practices is indicative of a number of factors, including financial success and political power. It's the equivalent of a crime lord attending church on a Sunday.

The causes vary from being humanitarian to being egotistic, political to environmental, economical to geographical. There are several realities that an aspiring off-gridder will have to confront, regardless of the reason(s) for moving off the grid in the first place.

First of all, unless you have the financial means to hire a builder to convert your house into its own self-sufficient utility, you are going to be required to make some adjustments to your way of life, acquire a great deal of technical information, and alter your typical daily activities. Among other things, this involves a significant emphasis on the preservation of energy. It's possible that living off the grid may cause shifts in your social patterns as well, which is particularly likely if you're relocating from one place to another. How do you cope when you're by yourself? If you find yourself moving to a place that is grid-tied, do you think you will be able to adjust to the cultural nuances of the new community as well as its perspectives on living a sustainable lifestyle? Will the fact that you are the

Off Grid Living

odd one out in the community worry you? On the other hand, if you find yourself in an off-grid community, do you think you'll be able to fit in with a group of individuals who you would perceive to be peculiar?

Second, you have to have some money. You will never be able to live off the grid if you are the kind of person who will never own land or a house and who is wholly reliant on the support of other people for your way of life. And the more severe the weather is where you live, the higher the expense of living off the grid will be for you. That doesn't mean you can't work on certain projects that are rather modest but nonetheless highly helpful. When the power grid is down, for instance, a backup hybrid solar/ generator system can be a lot of fun to construct and doesn't cost that much money. It will provide you with emergency lighting and allow you to continue using your television, computer, and refrigerator. From a different point of view, you may accomplish a lot just by remaining connected to the power grid and becoming a master in the art of energy saving. You will end up spending less money on it, saving more money, and putting less pressure on the electrical system.

Third, you will never be totally disconnected from the outside world. You either get about by driving a vehicle (with petrol costing over $5 per gallon) or riding a bike on a network (a grid) of roads that transport you to and from your place of employment, school, or church as well as the market. These are all areas that are organized according to the grid. All of your off-grid equipment is manufactured in facilities connected to the grid, and it is carried by grid-dependent vehicles powered by fossil fuels. Even while you may be producing the energy that is used to power your television and satellite receiver, the programming that you are really getting is coming from a grid. The Internet connection is also wireless. In the end, the money that you spend to acquire the necessities for your off-grid living comes from a job that depends on the grid. Get over it. Without any form of framework, life just cannot exist.

This book is for those individuals who have a real interest in off-grid initiatives and who sincerely want to have a good influence not only on their own lives but also on the lives of the people they love. There is no hyperbole involved here. Not to overstate things. No product endorsements. There are no elaborate do-it-yourself plans involved. No guarantees. Just some straightforward, uncomplicated information along with some pointers on where else you might get similar content.

Places to Start

You've already accomplished a lot by making the decision to live off the grid. You are looking for genuine freedom and independence in the life experiences you have. Your initial thought was presumably on where in the United States you should begin your off-grid living. This question undoubtedly sprang to mind right away.

Although it is possible to live off the grid in practically any part of the United States, there are some regions that are more ideal than others. There are many other aspects to take into account, including the following:

- **The weather as well as the climate**
- **Prices of land**
- **Building regulations specific to the area**
- **Taxes on real estate**
- **Legality**

Off Grid Living

Let's talk about the practical aspects of living off the grid in everyday life.

Water

As long as you don't waste it, there is enough water for every off-grid in North America in the form of groundwater and precipitation. This is true despite the effects of global warming and the droughts we've had over the last decade.

Some people have the good fortune to live in close proximity to bodies of water, such as lakes and streams, from which they may readily draw water using gravity, siphon systems, or pumps. Others of us aren't quite as fortunate, so over the following dozen or so pages, we'll discuss the steps we may take to ensure that we receive our fair share.

In the primary residence, I maintain, which has three occupants, I use around five gallons of water each day for cooking and drinking. Perhaps double that for doing the dishes and the washing, and then another two times that for tending to the garden and making sure the xeric landscaping stays in good shape. On the other hand, my neighbor gives her vast grass and wooded environment a full-bore watering for as long as twenty hours a day. It seems especially wicked in light of the fact that the drought in southeast Utah is still turning the land into ash and dust. "Since it's well water, I can do whatever I want with it," was her answer to my protests. "The Lord will provide for you."

The following is what the United States Geological Survey has to say regarding water being wasted by those who utilize wells: If you possess a water-table well and pump an excessive quantity of water from it, there is a risk that your well could run dry as consumption rates continue to rise and groundwater levels continue to drop. Because aquifers may cover a large area, the use of your well can have an effect on individuals who live hundreds or thousands of miles away. In times of low flow, the groundwater that feeds your well is also used to feed streams; thus, pumping from your well may also cause the water levels in streams to decrease. It's high time we stopped hoarding water like it's gold. The planet is struggling to provide for a massive and rapidly growing population. Your access to well water does not give you permission to be wasteful to an endless degree.

Efforts Made to Save Water

Several different strategies for water conservation are discussed in the chapter that I wrote on preserving natural resources. Permit me to highlight a few key elements here:

➢ Fewer flushes.
➢ Urgently repair any faucets or toilets that are leaking water.
➢ It is recommended to only wash full loads of clothes.

- ➤ If you want your plants and landscapes to look their best, use water that has been filtered or treated.
- ➤ Don't overwater.

Wells

Since we are already discussing this, why don't we speak about wells? A hole that has been excavated down to the water table or an aquifer (for explanations of these terms, see the glossary), as well as a pump or another mechanism that is used to extract the water from the hole. Just like every other aspect of life, wells are subject to stringent oversight from several departments of municipal and state government, most notably the health department. A poorly constructed well may allow harmful chemicals to seep into the surrounding water system. In addition, sinking a well is often an expensive endeavor, and you will probably want to dig a deep well since doing so increases the likelihood that you will find water that is actually free of impurities. Even if that happens, you should still consider purifying the water just to be safe. The moral of the story is that you should choose a qualified well-driller and ensure that the job is done correctly. Also, while determining how and where to dig your well, get the advice of the local farmers and those who have lived in the area for longer.

If you are fortunate enough to have access to the ideal location for drilling a well—for example, a water table 20 feet down, in deep loam or sandy clay with few rocks and no nearby contamination potential—it is quite possible to hand-drive the well. There are a few disadvantages to this method, however. The following is the procedure: Find a location that is as near to the home as you can get so that you can reduce the amount of pumping that has to be done between the well and the house. The location must be at least one hundred feet uphill and at least one hundred feet away from any potential source of pollution, such as an outhouse, animal stables, or septic systems. Employ a 1.25- to 2-inch well point as necessary (drive point). A pipe that is typically between 18 and 60 inches in length and has apertures that are big enough to let water in is referred to as a good point. The sediment matrix that is retaining the water determines the size of the holes that are there. The more finely ground the silt is, the more precise the hole size must be. Holes should admit smaller particles in but keep big particles out.

Use a maul to drive the well head into the ground as deeply as possible. When you need more length, remove the hammering cap, clean the threads, and screw on a new riser pipe using some monkey wrenches and a little joint or pipe thread compound in the threads. The new riser pipe should be between five and six feet in length and have a nipple that is six inches in diameter. Begin to pound the object once again, then carry out the procedure once more. During this procedure, you may need specialized drive couplings in order to deflect the impact away from the threads.

There is a large number of websites that provide advice on how to determine whether or not the tip of your well has penetrated water-bearing Earth. If you get close enough to an artesian source that has some pressure, you may find that water starts to spray up through the pipe. In such a case, you'll need to install a suction pump in order to bring the water to the surface.

It is feasible to dig a well with a hand-turned auger on soil that does not contain any rocks; however, this method requires a significant amount of manual work. A powerhead may be used to drive post-hole augers, and pressured water can be used to soften and clean out the hole while the augers work.

Off Grid Living

It is important to keep in mind that the hand-drawing technique may be used to extract water from a well even if the well is deeper than 200 feet. On the other hand, a suction pump will not function with water that is located more than twenty feet below the surface. In order to pump water from deeper wells, you will most likely utilize either a windmill or a submerged push-type electric pump (which might be supplied by solar or wind energy).

In times past, the customary method of building a well was first hand-digging a broad shaft and then completing the process using a windlass. This procedure is not feasible nor secure, particularly in circumstances in which the shaft is deeper than the diggers are tall and the Earth is unconsolidated. The caving in of shafts is a prevalent risk. Consult with knowledgeable people and get their opinion.

Springs

An upwelling of water at the surface of the Earth is what we refer to as a spring. This includes natural or artificial seepages from neighboring collectors that are just a few centimeters deep (including lakes, streams, aquifers, saturated sediment, and waste dumps). If you plan on drinking the water from the stream, you have an absolute obligation to have it thoroughly examined in a laboratory. The good news is that natural sediments and the organisms that live in the soil perform a great job of keeping water pure. The bad news is that they may become overwhelmed if they are subjected to excessive or frequent pollution. The presence of pollutants in the results of your test may indicate that you need to switch sources or delve deeper to find healthier water. There is a possibility that pesticides from the farm next door were used, and the presence of E. coli or an increase in phosphates indicates that the water was contaminated with sewage.

Finding a spring is often less difficult than it first seems to be. When there is a lot of snowmelt or a lot of rain, which may be found in the early spring months, then is the best time to search. Keep an eye out for little runnels that terminate in roadside ditches or other normally dry canyons or arroyos, and then trace them back to where they began. Visit this page on a regular basis to track the development of the neighborhood's flora. There is a spring there if it stays green throughout the year or if the Earth stays moist throughout the year. There are a lot of springs that really just seep.

If you reside in a region that is heavily forested, you should search the ground for deep, broad ruts. This seems to point to the existence of a waterway of some type, either above or below ground. A muddy basin or a tiny pond will form wherever there is a seep. There must be a spring in that area since there are plants typical of marshes growing in the black soil. It doesn't really matter whether the marsh smells bad since you're going to have the water tested no matter what, and odor isn't always an accurate indication of how contaminated the water is.

Once the spring has been identified, it has to be cleaned out and prepped. Before digging out the sluggish silt, it is simpler to wait till the surrounding region has reached its driest state first (which, again, may have an unpleasant smell). The water that nourishes the spring originates either from subsurface saturation or from subsurface flows in the deeper sediment or fissures in the bedrock. Both of these processes may cause the deeper sediment to become saturated with water. The goal here is to dig down far enough to reach this pristine water supply. After that, gravel and a pipe with holes in it are laid down in order to collect the water, and then a dam made of compacted dirt, plastic sheeting, or concrete is created downstream of the source in order to push the water into the pipe. The pipe is led to a spring box in order to collect the water, let the sand and debris settle, and prevent the water from being contaminated.

The following are some easy-to-follow recommendations that will assist you in maintaining the spring:

➤ Ensure that cattle and any other possible sources of pollution and contamination are kept away from the spring.

➤ By excavating, diversion ditches a good distance uphill from the box and divert surface water away from it. Surface water may include sediments that might contaminate the area.

➤ It is recommended that the settling basin be cleaned at least once every season, preferably twice per year.

- Repair any cracks or leaks in the spring box or the pipes.
- Do not let the overflow pipe get obstructed in any way.

How do you wind a spring after you have it in your possession? The simplest method is to use a bucket, but the majority of us feel that this is too severe. In the event that the spring is situated at a higher elevation than the home, the water may be transported to the house using a gravity-flow system and stored in a font, a cistern, or a water tank. Overflows of clean water from the font, cistern, or tank should be able to drain back into the streambed via a drain that has been designed appropriately. If you stack bales of hay or straw (or even soil) on top of the box, this can help keep it from freezing. Additionally, if you let some water drain from the box, this will delay the freezing process.

Catchment systems allow for the collection of precipitation.

A water catchment system, also known as a surface-water containment system, a rain-harvesting storage system, or a runoff catchment system, is an appealing option in situations in which groundwater is polluted, wells cannot be drilled, springs cannot be discovered, or rainfall is insufficient. These kinds of water management methods have been in use for thousands of years in regions of the world that have limited access to groundwater resources. Even in arid environments, even a brief rainfall may bring in sufficient water to keep a family functioning normally until the next significant storm.

The most typical method of rainwater collection is a rain barrel, which receives its supply of water from the downspout of the rain gutters or the eaves of the building. A wide variety of commercial rain barrels, some of which come equipped with their own roof-cleaner diverters, are available for purchase (they divert the roof water until the roof has been rinsed off). By the way, it seems that roofs made of metal or clay tiles are cleaner than roofs made of shingles. Before the water is allowed to reach the storage device, the system should feature a roof-cleaner diverter and maybe also a pre-filter if the water will be collected from a shingled roof.

The water that comes from a barrel is not under any kind of pressure, but it may be utilized to irrigate a garden by attaching a hose to the drain on the barrel. The pressure may be increased somewhat by elevating the barrel (often on cinder blocks), but without a pump, the pressure won't be sufficient to sustain any form of the plumbing system. Pumping, filtration, and disinfection systems are going to be required in order for stormwater harvesting systems to be able to deliver water that can be used for drinking, cooking, and bathing.

The harvesting system may also drain into bigger above-ground tanks, into below-ground cisterns, or into dammed reservoirs; some commercial versions of these reservoirs also feature roof cleaners. Alternatively, the system may drain into a combination of these three locations.

In addition to roofs, meltwater and precipitation may be collected from gullies and washes; nevertheless, the most visible concern is the accumulation of silt (mud), as well as the management of raging floods. Anything that lies farther downstream might be put in danger by large systems like this one.

A cistern is essentially nothing more than a tank, which may be constructed of concrete, steel, fiberglass, or plastic and can be positioned either above or below the Earth. You may get water pressure from the weight of the water in the cistern if the cistern or water tank is above ground and higher than the plumbing within your building. This is only possible if the cistern or water tank is higher than the piping. In any other case, you will need to utilize a pump in order to transport the water from the catchment to the home. Before the water can be used for drinking, cooking, or bathing, it must first go through a filtration process and then be disinfected.

Remember to take preventative measures to ensure that your rain barrel or any other above-ground storage item does not get frozen solid when you use it.

This 33-gallon trash can collector operates a length of the downslope soaker hose that is between 50 and 75 feet for roughly three hours. The hole on the top of the lid is used to collect runoff, and the gutter drain is inserted into the hole. The mosquitoes are prevented from multiplying thanks to the screen that is located under the lid. The hose may be switched on and off using the valve that is located at the bottom of the device. The price is $18, excluding the cost of the hose.

Putting Your Water to the Test

Before you consume any water obtained off the grid, make sure you test it first. If you are unable to test the water beforehand, you can treat and purify it by using a combination of the following methods: water treatment tablets purchased from a nearby sporting goods store or household bleach (sodium hypochlorite, 3 to 6 percent), added in the proportion of 1 teaspoon per 5 gallons of water.

The samples that are brought into the laboratory to be analyzed for chemicals and microorganisms, including Giardia cysts, have to be current (less than twenty-four hours old). Make use of a third-party testing firm to carry out the examinations. The all-inclusive examination will set you back a couple of hundred dollars. Although the local health department will be able to have the tests done at a lower cost, it could be a bad idea to include the HD in the process. If you are unsuccessful in stopping them, it may be quite difficult to remove them from the situation as "uninvolved."

Water-Source Hygiene

Pay attention to what is going on in the area around your water supply and the watershed that it comes from. Be on the lookout for contaminated chemicals, dead animals, and sewage from humans. Filter your water. It is a good idea to install a filter/chlorinator system at the wellhead and purifiers on or in front of the faucets that will be used for drinking and cooking water. Both of these steps should be considered. When it comes to filters, the quality of the product is often proportional to the cost. You should be prepared to spend some money on a decent system, and you should also be aware that high-tech filtration systems need regular testing of the water and the replacement of their filters.

Heating systems for the water

The majority of homes in the United States use water heaters of the storage or tank-type kind. They typically have a capacity ranging from 20 to 80 gallons, and they may be powered by electricity, propane, oil, or natural gas. These appliances heat water in a tank that is covered with insulation and provide a substantial quantity of water in a relatively short length of time. The fact that these devices continue to use energy even after they are turned off is one of their major drawbacks. The average lifespan of a tank is between ten and fifteen years; however, this lifespan may be extended by changing the internal anode rod of the tank.

Heaters that Use Heat Pumps

In order to move heat from one location to another, these machines make use of a heater/compressor and a fluid that acts as a refrigerant. They are powered by electricity, but the heat they produce comes from the air that is already heated in the area around the heat pump. Warm environments are optimal for the operation of heat pumps for this same reason. They use less power as a result of the fact that it requires less energy to transport heat around than it does to generate it. You may have them with water tanks already built in, which are termed integral units, or as add-ons to water heaters that you already have. Due to the high cost and level of difficulty involved in their installation, it is recommended that you employ a professional for this task.

Water heaters that work indirectly

The boiler from the central heating system is used by indirect water heaters. A separate tank that is insulated is used for the storage of hot water. A compact circulation pump and heat exchanger are responsible for the movement of heat away from the boiler.

The fact that it is an essential component of the heating system for the house and that it is often simplest to install when a new structure is being constructed by a contractor are both considered to be disadvantaged.

Heaters That Are Either On-Demand Or Tankless

These heaters will not begin operating until the water has been switched on and a certain minimum flow rate has been reached. When water moves through a heat exchanger that is similar to a radiator, a gas flame or a heater element is activated, which heats the water. The heated water is not stored in these heaters. There are a variety of possible safety features that could be included in tankless water heaters. A few examples of these features include temperature and pressure-relief valves, additional heat sensors on the heat exchanger, and a certain flow rate that must be met before the device will turn on.

The ability of the gadget to generate heat places a restriction on the flow rate itself. It allows for a restricted amount of gallons per minute of hot water to flow, and any increase in the flow rate causes the temperature of the water to drop. When the rate of consumption is average, the hot water supply will be depleted only when either the gas or the water is exhausted. The majority of models run on either natural gas or propane as their fuel source. There are electric variants available. However, they use a significant amount of power. This particular model of water heater is recommended for use in homes that are on the smaller side.

Solar heaters for the water

Solar water heaters (SWH) may be somewhat expensive, but the return on investment is often quite rapid. In general, they tend to be around three times as efficient as photovoltaic systems when it comes to gathering and processing the energy that comes from the sun. There is more than one kind of solar water heating system, and their operation varies greatly depending on the weather conditions. It's better to keep things straightforward. All of the sensors, valves, bells, and whistles have a propensity to malfunction. Passive designs, which utilize sunshine and heat as the primary controls, are used in basic heaters.

Getting Started with the Use of Solar Energy to Heat Water

1. Learn how to reduce your energy consumption.

2. Reduce the amount of energy you lose by increasing the number of appliances in your home that are energy-efficient while simultaneously lowering the amount of electricity you use overall.

3. Insulate your hot-water pipes as well as the jacket that covers your water heater to prevent heat loss.

4. Fix immediately any hot-water faucets that are leaking.

Many of today's textbooks give the impression that solar water heating is a very difficult process. This book's goal is to provide information on the options that are accessible to the general public while also offering an easy-to-understand explanation of various concepts. First, I'll explain the fundamental terminology (most of which was previously presented in chapter 5); next, I'll provide a quick description of the typical components of SWH systems; and finally, I'll describe the systems themselves.

The Fundamental Vocabulary Used in Solar Water Heating Systems

Comparing active and passive systems, active ones have some kind of moving components (like pumps and valves). Systems that are considered passive do not have any moving components.

A heat exchanger is a device that moves heat from one fluid to another by transferring it across a wall that conducts electricity.

The combining of a collector and a storage tank into a single unit (also known as a "batch") is referred to as an integrated collector storage system (ICS).

Comparing open-loop and closed-loop systems, open-loop systems (also known as direct systems) allow the collector to heat the domestic water directly, whereas closed-loop systems do not. A heat transfer fluid known as a solar fluid is heated by the collector in closed-loop systems, which are also frequently referred to as indirect systems. The heat is then transferred from the solar fluid to the domestic water via a heat exchanger.

This is the fluid that is utilized throughout closed-loop or indirect solar energy systems. Solar fluid. In most cases, it consists of distilled water or a mixture of antifreeze and water.

The word "thermosiphon" is a fancy one that refers to the natural convective flow of a liquid that occurs as a result of changes in temperature. Because of this, water or solar fluid can move around in a circuit without the need for a mechanical pump, as you will see in the following section.

Solar water heating system components and their functions.

The following is a list of components that may be found in SWH systems:

- collector
- mount for collectors
- storage tank
- water pump
- échangeur de Chaleur
- expansion tank
- controls
- isolation valves and temperature control valves
- emergency water heating system

It is important to keep in mind that not all components are essential for every system. The less complicated a system is, and the fewer components it has, the lower the risk of individual component failure will be, and the easier it will be to keep the system in good working order.

Collectors

Integrated Collector Storage (ICS) Devices, sometimes referred to as Batch Collectors.

In these types of setups, the solar absorber is the water tank that stores hot water. The tank is installed within an insulated box that is typically approximately 6 inches deep and has glass on one side. Additionally, the tank may be painted black or have a unique coating. The very bottom of the tank is supplied with ice water through a conduit. When the sun shines through the glass, it heats up the surface, which in turn warms the water that is contained inside the tank. When a hot faucet is turned on, water is drawn from the top of the tank to be used, and when the faucet is turned off, water is drawn from the bottom of the tank to be used. Some of them are single huge tanks that are at least 30 gallons in capacity, while others make use of many metal tubes that are connected to one another in a series. Steel is the typical material used for single tanks. Copper is the typical material used to make tubes. The performance of tube-type tanks is superior since more surface area is exposed; however, these tanks also get cooler at night more rapidly. On a bright sunny day, the inside of an ICS tank may become as hot as 180 degrees Fahrenheit, but on a warm overcast day, the temperature is only about half as high.

Batch collectors do not come without their share of drawbacks. When completely loaded, they become incredibly heavy and must be placed on very stable structures (a reinforced roof or on the ground). When installed, the collectors need to have a tilt to ensure that water can flow freely out of them. Batch warmers are helpful tools to have in places that seldom experience freezing temperatures. During the warmer months, they may be utilized in vacation homes, but the water has to be emptied before the ground freezes.

Collectors Using Flat Plates (FPCs)

Flat plate collector heaters are the kind that is used the most frequently everywhere in the world. They are long-lasting and efficient, and they prevent snow and ice from accumulating. FPCs are sturdy rectangular boxes that are normally four feet by eight feet and four to six inches deep. They have glass on the front of the collector and a solid rear. An absorber plate with copper pipe manifolds that run across the top and bottom of the collector within the frame may be found just under the glass. The frame itself contains the collector. A series of shorter riser tubes are welded in a perpendicular orientation along the manifold at intervals of about 4 to 5 inches. For the purpose of transferring heat from the fin to the riser, a flat copper fin is welded or soldered to the riser. In order to achieve the highest possible level of absorption, the fin is either painted or coated with a specialized substance. To be able to endure heavy winds, FPCs need a sturdy mount, which is often made of aluminum. To prevent corrosion, it is essential that each component of the collection be crafted out of a metal that is compatible with the others.

When it comes to the glazing of FPCs, low-iron, low-glare tempered glass is typically used. A rubberized gasket along the edge of the frame protects the frame while also ensuring that a proper seal is created.

The Valley of the Gods Bed and Breakfast has a system that uses evacuated tubes to provide hot water to the owners' room as well as the other four guest rooms.

Collectors for Evacuated Gases in Tubes (ETCs)

Inside of an ETC, each individual pipe or absorber plate has a vacuum tube made of annealed glass around it. The vacuum makes it possible for temperatures to rise to greater levels. In some configurations, the tube is linked to a manifold so that water may flow continuously through it. Other tubes hold a unique fluid that is capable of evaporating and traveling upwards to a heat exchanger. As the temperature drops, the moisture in the air condenses, and it then drips back into the tube. Still, other tubes have a metal rod attached to the absorber and protruding from the tube. This rod is meant to be inserted into a manifold, which is where the heat is picked up by circulating water.

One of the drawbacks of ETCs is that they are capable of producing temperatures that are higher than the boiling point of water (causing scald injuries and system-pressure hazards). These issues can be alleviated to some degree by utilizing a drain-back system, increasing the size of the storage tank, or decreasing the size of the collector (see below). The tubes are quite delicate, and the collectors do not do a good job of shedding snow and ice.

Collectors That Focus Their Energy

These make use of a reflecting parabolic surface to focus energy on a focal point in the device, which is where the absorber is situated. In order for the collector to be effective, it must follow the sun. Although it is capable of reaching high temperatures, the technology required to use it in home water heating systems is not currently available.

Collectors of the Pools

To put it plainly, the topic of swimming pools is not covered at all in this book. Participating in technology that operates independently from the grid allows one to meet the requirements of daily life. If you already own a swimming pool, you can afford to speak with a specialist, consultant, or dealer about the possibility of using solar energy to heat your pool. In the meanwhile, go to your search engine and key in "solar pool heaters." This will bring up a number of websites that will provide you with the fundamental information that you want to get started.

Mounts for Collectors

Mounting systems for collectors, sometimes known as racks, may be attached to a vehicle's roof, awning, or ground, depending on the kind of installation desired. Roof mounts are often installed on brackets that are a few inches above the roof and run parallel to it. In their most basic form, ground mounts consist of four posts whose lengths may be modified to accommodate tilt. Awning mounts are designed to connect the collector to a wall and make use of vertical supports in order to tilt the collector outward. When full of fluid or water, collectors can be an incredible amount of weight. Ground mounts are the most convenient option and the one that is least likely to result in structural damage to the house when weight is an issue.

Solar Storage Tanks

An insulated water tank is what's known as a solar storage tank. The water that comes out of your water heater is preheated by the sun, while the water that goes into it is cold. In closed-loop systems, the water is heated by coming into contact with a coil of pipe that rotates through the collectors and contains water or antifreeze. In open-loop systems, the water flows unimpeded through the collectors as it is continuously recirculated. After that, the water that has been heated by the sun is piped into the water heater's backup heating system, which is located on the water heater's cold side. When one of the hot water taps in the house is turned on, water that has already been warmed is transferred from the solar tank to the backup heater.

Water Pump

It is necessary for the water in a system to move in some way, and this can be accomplished either by a natural process (such as convection, gravity, or natural pressure) or by a mechanical pump (or circulator). To transfer water or antifreeze from the collector to the storage tank, either an electric (plug-in) or a solar-powered (direct current) pump may be employed. The distance that separates the collector and the tank, in addition to any elevation differences, determines the capacity of the pump. Pumps that are mechanical are not used in passive systems (batch and thermosiphon systems).

Heat Exchanger

This is a device that transfers heat from one fluid to another inside a closed-loop system without causing the fluids to mix. Some heat exchangers in storage tanks are installed internally, meaning inside the tank itself. These heat exchangers are typically nothing more than a coil of metal tubing or pipe situated at the tank's base. Alternately, the heat exchanger could be installed externally, wrapping around the outside of the tank and hidden by the insulation and cover. A common configuration for an external exchanger is a series of pipes within pipes, with water flowing in one direction and solar fluid flowing in the opposite direction. Either a pump or a thermosiphon (convection) process—or a combination of the two—is used to generate the flow.

Expansion Tanks

A bladder or diaphragm may be used to hold air in an expansion tank. The owner of the system decides on a certain operating pressure for the system. Solar fluid is pumped through the pipes and into the system. This fluid has a very specific volume and operates only within a narrow temperature range. The tank will make up for the fact that the fluid is becoming hotter and expanding by enabling the fluid to compress the air that is contained in the bladder or the diaphragm. This will ensure that the fluid pressure remains at an acceptable level. The system does not burst despite the temperatures being close to boiling, and the neighborhood is still enjoying a wonderful day despite the conditions.

The volume of liquid that the system transports dictates the size of the tank that must be used (the number and size of the collectors and the length and diameter of the pipes in the solar loop). The average household uses between three and six gallons of water each day. In most cases, a tank with a capacity of 2 gallons (#15) is enough for use in the house (a tank with a capacity of #30 has double the capacity). In order to function properly, closed-loop systems need expansion tanks.

Differential Controls

When the collector is hotter than the tank, active systems include a pump that circulates fluids throughout the system. However, the pump has to be turned off if the tank's temperature is higher than that of the collector. The differential control is responsible for ensuring that this is the case. There are a few various tools and methods that may be used to attain this goal. A differential thermostat does a temperature comparison between the collector and the tank and turns the heating or cooling system on and off appropriately. A PV pump is more straightforward: When the sun comes out, it starts working, and as the brightness of the light increases, the pump goes through its cycles at a higher rate. The pump will be turned off after the sun goes set. In batch or thermosiphon processing, differential controls are not required for any reason.

Isolation Valve (Solar Bypass)

This kind of bypass valve may be installed to isolate the solar tank in the event that there is an issue, or it can be used to bypass the backup water heater in the event that the solar water heater is capable of meeting all of the requirements of the home. By adjusting the position of the valve, the flow can be redirected to go around the solar tank or the backup heater.

When utilized, one or more are inserted in the incoming and outgoing lines to the water tank. This is done so that the solar tank may be isolated. The valve or valves nevertheless enable the emergency water heater to continue to function normally.

It is possible for an isolation valve to have either a three-port, two-valve configuration or a three-port, two-valve design.

Tempering Valve

A tempering valve, also known as a mixing valve, is installed at the very end of the system, just before the faucet, to protect users from becoming scalded. When the water reaches a certain temperature, the valve will open to allow cold water to be added. Directly on the valve, the user can adjust the temperature to their liking to achieve the desired effect.

Emergency Water Heater as a Backup

This heater can operate on a variety of fuels, including natural gas, propane, electric, and even wood. It does this by increasing the temperature of either water that has been preheated by the sun or water that has not yet been heated to the desired level. This makes it possible to have hot water regardless of whether or not the sun is shining. The backup heating option might be either a tank or a tankless system.

Several Distinct Categories of Solar-Powered Water Heaters

Put some serious thought into this since things are about to become more difficult from here on out. If you feel like you need a refresher on basic physics, I recommend that you read chapter 4 once again.

Batch (ICS) Systems

Batch (ICS) systems are the simplest, least costly, and easiest to implement of all the available options. These open-loop, passive, direct-heating systems are often placed in between a traditional water heater and a source of cold water. When a hot-water faucet is turned on, cold water enters the batch collector. This causes the batch collector's hot water to be forced out of the collection and into the secondary water heater. Only the amount of heat necessary to reach the temperature that has been set by the owner is added by the backup system.

It's possible that all you need for the most comprehensive batch system is a batch collector and some pipes. DIY instructions can be found all over the internet for making crude batch collectors, which are quite simple devices to construct.

Systems for Thermosiphoning (TS)

Convective currents are the engines that power these systems. To put it another way, heat rises, which results in a current being created. It is possible to utilize an open-loop TS in climates that are mild; this kind of TS involves cold household water being pumped into the bottom of the collector and then rising to the top of the collector as the water warms up. In regions with a colder temperature, a solar closed-loop system may employ an antifreeze solution that also contains water. Since it is probable that the collector will be located on the roof, it is possible to use a pipe that is resistant to freezing temperatures (such as PEX, which is cross-linked polyethylene) both on the roof and in the attic. Because the heated water is held in a tank that has enough insulation, there is no loss of heat during the nighttime hours.

Open-Loop Direct Systems

The most straightforward of the active system types is the open-loop direct kind. Regrettably, they can only be utilized in climates where the ground does not freeze solidly. The system is made up of a large solar collector as well as a substantial storage tank. Most of the time, a regular water heater tank is used, but the heating element is not connected to it. The backup water heater receives its supply of heated water from the storage tank, which also holds the preheated water. Before the system is started, the air in the collector is purged through either an automatic or manually operated air vent that is installed at the highest point of the collector. The water or fluid may be moved with the assistance of the circulating pump, which may be a simple PV pump rated at 10 watts or an AC (plug-in) pump equipped with thermostatic control. Installing something in the tank known as a snap-switch sensor allows one to set a maximum temperature for the space. This spring-loaded mechanism detects a certain temperature, at which point it snaps (rotates) ninety degrees, breaking the circuit and putting an end to the pump's operation.

Systematization of Pressurized Solar Fluid (Glycol)

The systems in question are active closed-loop configurations. The water that is used for household purposes goes to a storage tank rather than a collector. A combination of water and antifreeze is pumped through the collectors, transferred to the storage tank, and passed through a pipe-coil heat exchanger before being pumped back through the collectors. The heat that is conducted from the coil to the household water causes it to become warmer.

The solar fluid that is circulated through the collector is often a mixture of water and glycol, which keeps the fluid from freezing. The warmer the environment, the lower the percentage of glycol that is utilized. Because antifreeze does have certain drawbacks in comparison to water, the amount that is utilized should be kept as low as it safely can be.

These kinds of systems need a storage tank for expansion in addition to other components for venting and routing. Their primary benefit is that the collector may be installed in any location without the risk of it being frozen.

Drainage-Back Systems With a Closed Loop

When a pump in these systems is activated, solar fluid, which is distilled water, is drawn from a reservoir (which is typically a 10-gallon drain-back tank), and then it is circulated through the flat plate or evacuated tube collector as well as the heat exchanger. When the pump is turned off, the solar fluid will begin to return to the reservoir where it was stored. When the pump is turned off, the collector is left empty. The collector is fed by a high-speed pump, and a differential temperature control determines when it should be turned on and off. Various ways are utilized to transmit heat from the drain-back tank to the solar storage tank. The downsides of this system are that the collector must be situated higher than the reservoir, and drain-back tanks are tiny and do not hold much heat. In warmer regions, drain-back systems function most effectively.

Food

Are you prepared to provide for the nutritional needs of your family with what you cultivate and raise? You should get started right away if you want to lessen your reliance on the food supplied by commercial businesses. It is essential to establish a farm that is capable of generating sufficient food for one's needs well in advance of when those needs may arise.

It takes time to establish crops, develop infrastructure, raise animals, and smooth out the kinks, and you may have to endure a few years of less success before you can really feed off the grid.

Assuming you have a home on the cleared property and at least one useful outbuilding already completed, you will be able to concentrate on cultivating edible plants after these conditions are met. Two people may cultivate enough food from the land in a few short years if they work it

Off Grid Living

diligently, pay attention to the changing of the seasons and the weather, use productive labor habits, and maintain a consistent work schedule. Taking into account the amount of time needed for planting, growing, daily chores, controlling pests and weeds, maintaining soil quality, and building a homestead, it is reasonable to expect a partially self-sufficient homestead within three years and a fully self-sustaining homestead within approximately five years. You should make preparations to have the following in addition to a milk supply, such as cows or goats:

1. Beans – Beans are a dependable and simple crop to cultivate, making them an essential source of sustenance for a farming household. Early preparation of the soil and a growing period of at least two to three months before harvest is necessary to achieve a harvest in the first year, with an increase in yield anticipated in the following year.

Off Grid Living

2. Poultry: If you start with chicks, you should plan on spending at least two to three years successfully raising, selecting, brooding, and culling birds before you can consider your flock established. In the interim, you will gather eggs and consume the chickens and ducks that you have decided not to maintain as part of the flock. You should begin with 10–12 chicks, and you should aim to butcher them when they are around 3–4 months old.

3. Rabbits - Rabbits are an efficient way to provide meat for your family in a short amount of time. It is not unrealistic to anticipate that a single breeding couple will produce twenty or more rabbits on an annual basis. It may take your bunnies anything from one to two years to get established. Breeding performance, overall health, and size should be selected, and new genotypes should be introduced on a regular basis.

4. Corn is a productive grain crop that must get a great deal of nourishment from the soil and must

be heated for a period of time equal to or more than four months. It is not rare for a person's first year of producing corn to have a significant amount of loss due to the weather, pests, or soil conditions. However, once these problems have been resolved, maize has the potential to become an essential staple crop. Expect to spend around two years learning the ropes before you can cultivate a considerable yield.

5. Wheat — Despite being one of the most widely consumed cereals in the United States, wheat is a somewhat difficult crop to cultivate and harvest. After about two months of hot weather, wheat is ready to harvest. Consider the amount of time necessary to thresh and grind the wheat while making your planting plans.

6. Winter Squash - If you want to offer your family critical vitamins and have an easy harvest to maintain over the winter, consider growing winter squash. Although it takes up to four months for

winter squash to develop, you should be able to achieve a fair crop in your first year of growing it if you control your pests well and water it enough.

7. Apples Despite the fact that apples have a wide range of applications, you will need to allow anywhere from six to ten years for your apple trees to produce fruit. However, having patience will pay off, and planting apple trees is an endeavor that is well worth the delay.

8. Potatoes — Beginning with potatoes is a simple process. Your first year growing potatoes should provide you with a respectable harvest. More season cultivars may take up to three months or longer to mature, but shorter season types may mature in as little as two months.

9. Honey Honey is a wonderful sweetener that can be used on the farm, and it also offers a number of health benefits. In addition, bees are important for agricultural pollination. However, it takes some time for bees to bring their output up to full speed.

Your harvest during the first year will be quite little, but by the second year, you should be able to collect up to 30 pounds of extra honey from a single hive (leaving the bees something to eat over the winter).

Start working on projects like this right now if being self-sufficient is what you want to achieve. Even if you still buy the majority of your food, it is still in your best interest to develop your homestead in a way that will allow you to gradually wean yourself off of doing so. This will ensure that you do not have to spend your early years of self-sufficiency scurrying around in search of food.

Growing Your Garden

Developing a strategy for your own and your family's survival in a world that is becoming more volatile is going to become an increasingly vital priority. There are whole books devoted to detailing the most effective methods for creating

Off Grid Living

shelters that are both secure and able to withstand adverse conditions, as well as stockpiling food and other essential supplies. However, as the amount of food that has been stockpiled starts to diminish, survivalists will need to know how to create food for themselves and how to live off the land in order to be successful. At this point, having a survival garden that has been well laid out becomes absolutely necessary.

Traditional gardening is something that a lot of people are already acquainted with, but if you want your garden to be able to provide you and your family enough food to keep you alive, you're going to need some more specialized knowledge. Make a mental note of these seven useful suggestions for creating a survival garden to sustain yourself and your family; this might be the difference between life and death.

1. Determine the place that best suits you.

Off Grid Living

Your survival garden, like any other garden, has to be located in a region that has circumstances that are ideal for plant growth. In order for a garden to be successful, the location must have enough drainage and be exposed to direct sunshine for at least six hours every day.

You may start planning the site of your survival garden and prepping the surroundings as soon as possible, which is something that you should do since we never truly know when an emergency scenario may come. There is no downside to having an excess of fresh food, and the knowledge you receive from producing your own food will serve you well in the future, so having a lot of it is not a problem.

2. Prior to selecting your plants, you should first take into account the temperature zones of your region.

The success of your garden will be strongly influenced by the climatic zones in your immediate area. Find out what kinds of plants will thrive in your region by consulting resources on the internet to determine your growth zone or talking to experienced gardeners in the neighborhood for their recommendations.

3. Make a plan for what you are going to cultivate and start a collection of seeds for future usage

Make a list of the various freshly produced foods that your family is willing to consume and include them on the list. Growing your own food in advance of an emergency scenario enables you to choose which kinds of food you and your family want to eat in the event of a crisis.

There are a variety of survival websites where you may buy seeds that have been specifically packed to keep for many years. You may also guarantee the longevity of seeds you get from other sources by keeping them in a place that is both cold and dry and in a container that cannot be opened by rats or other types of pests.

4. Do some research on healthy eating and living a long life.

If your garden ends up being a substantial source of food for your household, it is imperative that you cultivate crops that will fulfill a large portion of your family's dietary requirements. If you live in a location with a short growing season, it is very necessary to cultivate crops that keep well. There are certain items that should always be included in a survival garden, regardless of how much a particular household enjoys others.

Plants that provide the best possible nutrition:

- Beans
- Peanuts
- Potatoes
- Flowering sunflowers (for sprouts and seeds)
- Sweet potatoes
- Peas
- Squash
- Carrots

- Beets
- Cabbage
- Corn
- Tomatoes
- Berries
- Grapes

5. Plant herbs

Make sure to include some medicinal plants in your garden of survival. Herbs take up very little room and need very little in the way of specialized care, but they provide a wide range of health benefits and enhance the flavor of the food that you grow in your garden.

Be conscious of the fact that there are a variety of applications for these herbs that may be used to access the medical benefits they provide. You may seek the advice of local herbalists or make use of the resources available online if you want a complete guide on the medicinal qualities of these plants and others.

Must-have herbs for survival gardens:

- Basil
- Parsley
- Rosemary
- Chamomile
- Lemon Balm
- Thyme
- Echinacea (Purple Cone Flower)
- The milk thistle seed
- Lavender
- Chives
- Sage
- Dill
- Planting fresh herbs

6. Establish a method for the use of natural irrigation

There is a possibility that you will not have access to running water from your local supplier if the severity of the situation warrants it. Utilizing a rain collecting barrel as a source of water for your plants is the most straightforward method of doing so. Large barrels that are appropriate for collecting rainwater may be found in certain home improvement shops as well as online. Some websites even sell them.

Either use a number of smaller buckets to transport the water to the garden or attach a spigot, along with a hose, to the barrel before using it. Be careful to install a screen or some kind of mesh on the top of the rain barrel so that trash and insect larvae are kept to a minimum. In addition, the water that has been purified in this manner may be consumed or used in the preparation of food.

7. Fend off both animals and people as you tend to your survival garden.

If you are starving and require food produced in your garden to fend off death, it is probable that other people and animals in the area are also seeking food at the same time. Putting up a fence around your garden plot is one approach to prevent ravenous animals from getting inside, but it may not be enough to stop them.

If you have a dog or cat as a pet, collecting any loose hair from them and burying it near to the surface around the edge of the garden may scare away any animals that may be in the area. If you don't have access to pet hair, gardening websites and outdoor stores offer wolf urine, which is also effective in discouraging thieves from stealing from gardens.

It is more challenging to prevent people from entering your garden. It is recommended by a great number of survivalists that you grow a garden in such a manner that it does not resemble a garden at all and does not follow any particular structure. An effective method for disguising a garden is to let berry bushes and vegetables that grow on vines get slightly overgrown over time.

Off Grid Living

You should also try to hide any obvious evidence that you are cultivating food, such as keeping your gardening equipment out in the open. You have the ability to keep watch over your survival garden, but it's usually in your best interest to avoid getting into a fight over food.

It is always preferable to be prepared and ready in the case that your gardening abilities are the only thing that stands between you and famine, even if no one ever wants to be in a situation where they require a survivalist garden.

Conservation of Resources

Being off the grid has its perks, but let's face it: it forces you to adapt to your lifestyle. Perform a trial run of your off-grid living situation before investing thousands of dollars in the endeavor. While you are disconnected from the power grid, you should make every effort to reduce your energy use. You will benefit in several ways from this: To begin, you could discover that you can cut your monthly electricity expenditures by such a significant amount that living off the grid is no longer financially feasible for you. When it comes to the size of your alternative power systems, you will have the ability to make more precise predictions about the very minimum requirements that you will have. Third, it demonstrates that you are really committed to making a difference in the world and not merely putting up a religious front for the sake of impressing your contemporaries.

Off Grid Living

It is almost impossible to have a conversation on conservation without at some point bringing up catchphrases such as "carbon footprint," "greenhouse gases," and "global warming." The majority of people in the United States are completely unaware of what a carbon footprint is, and it is almost guaranteed that over the next few years, another phrase will emerge to take its place. But before we go into it, let's examine the idea. Your carbon footprint refers to the direct influence that your activities and way of life have on the environment in terms of the amount of carbon dioxide that is emitted. It is estimated that the typical American generates around 40,000 pounds of CO_2 emissions each year, and it is CO_2 that is mostly to blame for the contribution of humans to the phenomenon of global warming. Therefore, when I talk about these steps for energy conservation, I'm not only giving you a way to cut down on your monthly utility bills and practice your

Off Grid Living

off-grid lifestyle; I'm also giving you some concrete recommendations on how to significantly reduce the amount of carbon footprint left behind by your daily activities. It shouldn't be difficult to include these suggestions in the blueprints for your new house if you're in the process of constructing one. If you are currently living in the house that will be your permanent residence, you will discover that bringing it up to these requirements might be extremely expensive. Fortunately, the majority of these ideas will bring a rapid return in terms of lowering your monthly bills for utilities such as water and electricity.

Landscaping

You may keep your house cooler in the summer by planting several trees outside that provide shade in various parts of the yard. Make sure that bushes are kept at a safe distance from the vents of your air conditioner. Add to it some xeriscaping, which is a form of landscaping that helps to reduce the use of water. The following are some of the concepts that underlie it:

- You should do your planning and design depending on the climate of your location as well as the microclimate.
- Plants that are able to thrive in those climates should be zoned appropriately, and they should be selected appropriately (often native species considered to be weeds by your water-hogging neighbors).
- Reducing the amount of grass or turf that has to be heavily watered. It may be necessary, in some circumstances, for you to either let the grass on your lawn die naturally or to actively eliminate it so that it does not compete with the plants in your xeric garden.
- Soil improvement. A soil that has been improved has increased absorption as well as its ability to retain moisture. In addition to

providing critical nutrients, plants benefit from soils that have had organic matter added to them. Before installing watering systems, the land should have undergone a variety of changes, including tilling, grading, the addition of organics, and others.

➢ Irrigation or watering that is sufficient and effective. Do not overwater your plants; instead, figure out how much they really need, take into account evapotranspiration (the rate at which water evaporates from the soil plus the quantity that is lost via the plant's leaves), and then water them appropriately. The extension service in your area can provide you with the ET rate. If you need to water or irrigate your garden, do it first thing in the morning when evaporation rates are at their lowest. If you must use sprinklers, choose those that provide large droplets of water.

Before they can reach the ground, mists and droplets of rain are dispersed by the wind or evaporate due to the high temperature. Gravel is often recommended as an alternative to mulch by xeriscapers because of the fact that it may catch dew.

- ➤ Make use of compost and mulch in order to prevent the development of weeds, give nutrients, reduce the rate at which water evaporates, and maintain an enhanced soil.
- ➤ A sufficient amount of upkeep should include weed control, trimming, and insect control.

Home Appliances That Use Less Energy

When purchasing new home appliances, it is important to thoroughly inspect the yellow labels

Off Grid Living

that are part of the Energy Guide. These labels will inform you how efficient the appliance is with energy and will really show you how much energy the appliance consumes in comparison to other models that are the same or comparable. This is shown in a white box in the middle of the label, and it may begin with the phrases that describe this model... Energy Guide labels are required by the Department of Energy (DOE) to be placed on new appliances that have a fairly wide range of energy efficiencies between different models. Examples of these types of appliances include refrigerators, freezers, water heaters, dishwashers, clothes washers, air conditioners, heat pumps, and furnaces. The label is not needed to be shown on appliances such as kitchen ranges, clothes dryers, and microwave ovens since there is minimal variation in the amount of energy they use across different models.

Off Grid Living

ENERGY STAR is a second label that you might find on new home appliances. This label is part of a voluntary labeling program run by the Environmental Protection Agency (EPA) that aims to assist consumers in recognizing products that use less energy in an effort to lower greenhouse gas emissions from power plants. Home appliances that have the ENERGY STAR designation exceed the federal efficiency criteria. An appliance that is certified for the ENERGY STAR program will also carry the Energy Guide label. Energy Guide labels may occasionally indicate whether or not a device is eligible for the ENERGY STAR program. Use these labels to comparison-shop. Appliances that have a high level of efficiency often have a higher purchase price, but the money you save on your monthly energy bills will more than make up the difference over the course of the appliance's lifespan.

When purchasing new home equipment, it is important to think logically about all the bells and whistles that come with it. For example, refrigerators that defrost manually consume one-third less energy than those that defrost automatically.

Home Improvements

Include some kind of insulation. When insulating walls and ceilings in a newly constructed house, it is recommended that you go above and above the municipal standard. It will have a beneficial effect on both your heating and cooling costs. In addition to this, you should insulate the ducts and pipes that carry hot water and hot air throughout the home. Installing a fan in the attic that is controlled by a thermostat can help remove the hot air.

Typical windows should be replaced with argon-filled double-glazed or thermopane windows instead of single-glazed windows. The use of storm windows and doors considerably cuts down on the amount of heat that is lost. If you cover the window frame on the inside with clear plastic, you can accomplish the same thing; however, you should be careful when the weather gets warmer. The temperature difference between the glass and the plastic can cause the glass to crack if it is hit by cold rain, and it can melt any plastic that is trapped between the two layers. Commercially available reflective films have the ability to screen out heat without considerably diminishing the amount of light that can pass through or the view that can be seen outside. You should install some external awnings over the windows that face south. The drapes and blinds in the house will act as a thermal barrier for the residence.

You should paint your home in a hue that complements it. In cooler regions, darker colors are preferable because they are better at retaining heat, whereas lighter colors are more effective in reflecting the sun's rays in warmer climes.

To prevent air from escaping via doors, windows, and gaps in the walls, you can weatherize your house by applying caulk and installing weather stripping.

Lighting

In order to replace your outdated incandescent bulbs, you need to switch to using screw-in fluorescent lights. They use one-fourth as much power but have a lifespan that is about 10 times longer. If you really must use incandescent bulbs, be sure to choose the "energy saver" version. These bulbs are packed with halogen gas, which allows them to provide a brighter light while consuming less power.

If you want additional light, make sure the light fixtures in your home are clean. By painting the walls and ceilings in brighter hues, you may make use of the light that is reflected. It will take fewer watts to provide the same level of lighting if the light bulbs and fixtures are kept clean; this will also improve the quality of the reflected light.

You may reduce the number of watts you use by sitting down and drawing a map of the home to figure out how much lighting you need in each room. This is another fantastic way to save money. For instance, you may not need a lot of wattage in the corridors; you don't need to light up the whole living room; nevertheless, you may want more watts in the section of your kitchen where you cook or in the section of the living room where you sit to read. This kind of lighting is known as task lighting, and it denotes that although general spaces may have little or no illumination at all, sections that are specifically designed for a job or that pose a safety danger should have bright lighting.

Off Grid Living

It is not cost-effective to switch off fluorescent lights until you are out of the room for more than ten to fifteen minutes. This is because fluorescent lights need more power to start up. If, on the other hand, you have lights that are lit by incandescent bulbs, you should make it a point to switch them off whenever you leave a room.

Timers, photosensitive controls, and motion sensors are all examples of devices that may help you save money. Establish a schedule for when the lights should come on using a timer. When the sun goes down or when heavy clouds cover the sun, a photo control will turn the lights on. When the sun returns, the photo control will turn the lights off. When motion is detected by the sensors, the lights will automatically switch on. Motion detectors are put to use for the purpose of security the vast majority of the time, but they also have the potential to reduce your monthly power cost. The light stays on for a certain amount of time, and then it automatically shuts off again after that. It is preferable to the common practice of keeping the exterior security or entry lights on all night. Motion sensors are available in the form of entire fixtures, screw-in add-ons, or adapters. A large number of motion sensors are photosensitive or have a timer that causes them to switch off during the day.

Heating and Cooling of the Ambient Air

Check the filters in your central heating system and either clean them or replace them before they get clogged with dust and debris. During the winter, you should set your thermostat to the lowest temperature at which you are still comfortable (say, 68 degrees F in the daytime and 60 degrees overnight). When the sun is shining, open the blinds and curtains on the sun-facing windows, but be sure to keep them closed at night, so the warmth stays inside. Either put some pans of water at the tops of the radiators and warm vents or run a humidifier in the room. Dry air may make you feel colder, while humid air might make you feel warmer.

Every couple of years, you should have a heating system inspection performed by a qualified HVAC technician.

There are a number of compelling arguments to support the use of an air conditioner that is proportionately sized to the space that has to be cooled. If the space is too huge, the machine will cycle off and on repeatedly. If it is too tiny, it will run continuously throughout the day and possibly throughout the night as well since it will not be able to achieve a pleasant temperature in the area before sleep.

Place your air conditioner on the side of the house that gets the most shadow. When exposed to strong sunshine, an air conditioner's energy consumption will be higher than when it is operating in the shade. On hot days, closing the fresh-air intake will result in modest energy savings due to the recirculation of the precooled air within the building. Turn off the air conditioning in any rooms that aren't being used. If you are going to be gone all day, you may want to think about placing your air conditioner on a timer so that it won't turn on during the day but will still chill the house down before you return.

During the warm months, maintain a thermostat setting that is as high as you can bear the heat comfortably (say, 78 degrees). Fans may be of assistance, as they circulate air and make it possible for you to maintain the thermostat set at a slightly higher level, and in certain cases, they can even eliminate the need that you to use the air conditioner. Even the largest ceiling fans use just a tiny portion of the energy that is necessary to power an air conditioner.

When it's really hot outside, you should avoid doing anything that will add to the amount of moisture in the air, such as cooking, taking a shower, or doing the laundry. Carry out such responsibilities earlier in the morning or later in the evening, when it is less hot. Additionally, the usage of ovens and other equipment that generate heat should take place only in the early morning or late evening hours.

Every month, you should inspect the filter for your air conditioner and either replace it or clean it if it's unclean. Instructions on how to properly clean the condenser coils and fins may be found in the owner's handbook.

Refrigeration

Check to see that the door of the refrigerator or freezer closes securely. In such a case, you need either clean or replace the seal. Utilize a brush or vacuum to maintain the cleanliness of the condenser coils, which may be found in the rear or bottom of the refrigerator. If it has a switch for conserving energy, you should turn it on.

Keep the refrigerator and freezer away from hot rooms, the sun, heating vents, and other equipment that generate heat, such as ovens, dishwashers, and space heaters.

Maintain a full state in the freezer section, but do not obstruct the fan that drives the cold air circulation. When the freezer is full, it requires less electricity to maintain its frozen state. Water bottles should be used to fill any vacant area. In the event that the power should ever go out, they will assist in maintaining the temperature of the freezer, and you may move some of them into the refrigerator in order to maintain its temperature as well.

Keep the temperature of the refrigerator between 34 and 40 degrees Fahrenheit and the temperature of the freezer between 0 and 5 degrees. Anything below that point is a complete waste of effort. The only way to know for certain whether or not the temperature is safe is to place a thermometer in the storage area. They are inexpensive and may be purchased at any bargain retailer.

Laundry

Warm water should be used for garments that are substantially filthy, while cold water should be used for items that are just mildly soiled. Make sure you choose detergents that are formulated to work well in cold water. Everything should be washed in cold water. Rinsing garments in warm or hot water does not improve their cleanliness. Always wash a full load rather than a half load. If you are drying more than one load at once, be sure to complete each load immediately after the other. Don't give the dryer time to become cold in between loads. Be careful not to overdry loads. It is not only costly, but it also wreaks havoc on textiles. Dry both heavy and light materials in their own designated dryers. When they are combined, the total amount of time that the dryer is in operation will be extended. Before each load, you should always clean the lint filter. Drying times are lengthened when filters get clogged. Do you recall when people used to dry their clothes by hanging them outside?

Steaming Water

Reduce the temperature on your water heater to 120 degrees on the thermostat. Set the temperature on your dishwasher to 130 if it does not have a temperature booster. Reduce the temperature in the home before you go for many days if you plan on being gone for that long. You may put your electric water heater on a timer so that it only warms up the water during the hours in which you are most likely to use it, or you can set it to switch off altogether during the night. Both of these options are viable.

Either use an insulating blanket to wrap around your water heater or put some fiberglass insulation around it. Some more recent heaters already have insulation built in. Insulating the pipes that carry hot water is an excellent option, as was noted before.

As quickly as possible, fix any faucets that are dripping. In the shower, use a showerhead that has a flow control or a low-flow setting.

Dishwashing

Before filling the dishwasher, give the dishes a quick rinse in cold water, and don't turn it on until it has a full load. Think about letting the dishes air-dry before putting them away.

Cooking

Make use of the microwave. Your electric oven won't even come close to keeping up with its speed or efficiency when compared to this.

Off Grid Living

It is more efficient to cook many items in your standard oven at the same time and, as a result, at the same temperature. Do not open the door to check on the status of the situation. Simply opening the door will be enough to produce a noticeable temperature change.

Glass pans are superior to metal pans in terms of their ability to retain heat. When using glass, preheating periods may be cut in half, and temperatures can be reduced by 5 percent without sacrificing safety.

On the range-top, you should make use of pots and pans that have flat bottoms and that are the appropriate size for the burner. To reduce the amount of time needed for cooking, cook with the lids on the pans.

Off Grid Living

Transportation

Texts on sustainability and living off the grid almost often dedicate a significant amount of attention to discussing alternate modes of transportation. The reason for this is that it is said that the combustion of one gallon of gasoline will create 23 pounds of carbon dioxide. Despite the fact that the arithmetic doesn't really make much sense (a gallon of petrol only weighs 6 pounds), we get what you're trying to say. Not to mention the fact that the price of a gallon of gasoline was above $4 at the time that this article was written. There will come a day when we will no longer be able to purchase our automobiles that run on gasoline. Automobile manufacturers are now paying notice, and as a result, they are rushing to build electric and hybrid automobiles. Their success will be determined in large part by the development of suitable battery technologies, the emergence of technology for plug-in hybrid electric vehicles (PHEV), and the discovery of a market for alternative fuels such as ethanol, biodiesel, biogas, and hydrogen cell technologies. The long-term objective is to perfect automobiles that produce no emissions whatsoever by eschewing the combustion of fossil fuels in favor of the use of alternative fuels such as hydrogen.

The majority of Americans are not yet in a position to be able to afford hybrid or electric vehicles. For the time being, the individuals who have the greatest need for them will not be the ones to get them. While we wait, here are several activities that the common person may participate in:

- ➤ Be sure to choose a vehicle with good gas mileage.
- ➤ Make use of a motor vehicle that is capable of running on either ethanol or biodiesel (although mechanics are finding some problems in vehicles that use ethanol).
- ➤ Use public transportation.

Off Grid Living

➢ Carpool.

Generating Energy

In order for us to get through the following two chapters, we are going to have to go back and study everything that our teachers attempted to teach us back when we were in high school science class unless you are a physicist or an electronics technician. This is the information that caused all of us to ask one another, "Why in the world are they having us study this crap? This useless nonsense will never find a place in our actual life. Well, surprise! The answer is there in front of us, sneering at us like a haughty mother-in-law.

Energy is required for anything at all to take place, and whenever something does take place, energy is transformed from one form to another. Various kinds of energy each provide their own unique set of effects. Electrical energy, heat, light, sound, solar energy, chemical energy, kinetic energy, and potential energy are just a few of the various forms that energy may take. The term "chemical energy" refers to the energy that is produced as a byproduct of chemical processes. Chemical energy may be stored in a variety of different forms, including food (like the meal you had this morning) and fuels (such as coal, gas, and oil). Batteries are as well.

The energy that comes from motion is known as kinetic energy. When anything travels at a higher speed, it has a greater amount of kinetic energy; conversely, when it moves at a slower speed, it possesses a lesser amount of kinetic energy. When moving items collide with stationary ones, part of the kinetic energy of the moving objects is transmitted to the stationary ones, which in turn causes the stationary ones to move.

The energy that objects possess owing to their location in a force field, such as an electrical field, gravitational field, or magnetic field, is referred to as potential energy.

Off Grid Living

According to the principle known as the Law of Conservation of Energy, energy cannot be generated nor destroyed; yet, it may change forms. As was discussed before, anytime anything occurs that requires the expenditure of energy, that energy is transformed into a new form. Heat and light are the end products of the vast majority of energy transformations. Even these ultimate forms are not completely eradicated; rather, they are dispersed so widely over the ecosystem that it is impossible to make use of them. One example of this would be the energy chain that powers a flashlight. The batteries convert the chemical energy stored inside them into electrical energy. Within the light bulb, electrical energy is converted into light and heat, which are then released into the environment.

Even while we meet a significant portion of our immediate energy requirements by burning fuels, the vast majority of the energy we use on earth originates either directly or indirectly from the sun. In order for solar energy to reach Earth, it must first be converted into electromagnetic energy, a kind of energy that is capable of traversing vast distances. The sun is the source of the planet's heat. The sun provides the plants with the energy they need to produce food, which we then consume. In addition, the energy from the sun may be used to do things like heat water with a solar collector or create electricity with a solar cell.

Sources of energy that can only be utilized once to create energy are referred to as non-renewable energy sources. They include fuels such as coal, natural gas, oil, and other similar substances. The term "renewable sources of energy" refers to those that are not depleted over time (that is, they can be created at a rate higher than it is possible for humans to consume them, such as sunlight, wind, and flowing water), or that can be replicated on demand.

Off Grid Living

Over ninety percent of the world's energy requirements are met by the combustion of fossil fuels and wood. Fossil fuels are those that have been produced from the remnants of extinct plants and animals. The remaining is approximately divided into equal parts between energy derived from nuclear sources and energy derived from renewable resources.

As a consequence of the combustion of fossil fuels, huge quantities of carbon dioxide (CO_2), as well as other gases, are released into the atmosphere. Even Nevertheless, there are reasonable individuals who continue to reject that the greenhouse effect, global warming, and acid rain may be largely blamed on the intensive usage of fuels. This is the case even in the present day.

An intriguing example of a sustainable fuel is biogas. When organic matter decomposes, it creates a gas called methane, which may be used to heat both air and water. Additionally, it has been used in the propulsion of some autos and even jet planes. Even if it is produced from renewable resources, biogas is still combusted like any other fuel, which is one of its many drawbacks.

Other sources of renewable energy include wind and water, in addition to solar, which was just stated. Moving water spins turbines at a hydroelectric plant, which results in the generation of power. A wind farm is able to produce power because the wind turns the turbines, which in turn spin the propellers.

Energy through Heat

When a material takes in heat, it causes an increase in the amount of energy stored inside itself. The sum of the kinetic energy and the potential energy of the atoms that make up material is referred to as the substance's internal energy.

The transfer of heat from warm to cold things causes a shift in the total amount of energy contained in each of the original states. It will keep flowing until both of the items reach the same temperature. When a thing loses heat, it also loses some of its internal energy. Objects that warm up see an increase in their total internal energy.

Conduction, convection, and radiation are the three mechanisms that might be responsible for the passage of heat (also known as heat transfer).

In the process of conduction, heat is transported from one item to another by the molecular excitation that occurs inside a material, even while the object itself does not move. When excited particles collide with slower particles, the excited particles' energy is transferred to the slower particles, resulting in the transfer of energy.

Convection is a method of transferring heat that relies on the motion of a fluid or gas. When a gas or fluid is heated, it expands and loses density, becoming less dense and more buoyant than the gas or fluid that it is surrounded by. It moves away from the source of heat while simultaneously carrying energy with it as it ascends. Convection currents are created when cooler gas or fluid falls to the bottom of a space, creating a circuit of circulation.

Radiation takes place whenever heat is transported from one location to another by electromagnetic waves, which carry energy away from the source.

To increase the temperature of one kilogram (2.2 pounds) of water by one degree Celsius, the amount of energy required is 4,200 joules (1.8 degrees Fahrenheit). However, certain materials are far better at absorbing heat than others. To get the temperature of a mixture containing the same quantity of each substance up to the same level, more or less heat is needed. For instance, the amount of heat energy required to get a quart of water to a temperature of 100 degrees is more than the amount of heat energy required to bring a quart of oil to the same temperature.

Convection

The term "temperature" refers to how hot an object or substance is. Certain kinds of heat behave differently in various materials (thermal capacities). When heated with the same amount of energy, two masses of the same size but made of different substances, for example, a quart of oil and a liter of water, will each achieve a different temperature. The temperature of the oil will really be higher than that of the water. The disparity in heat capacity between land masses and bodies of water is what causes the land to heat up more quickly than water, which in turn creates sea breezes. The air that has been warmed by the land mass that is heating up more quickly rises, while the air that is coming in from the body of water is colder. When attempting to design buildings that are good at retaining heat, it is essential to have a solid understanding of the principles of thermal capacity and heat transport.

There are a few different scales that may be used to measure temperature. The Fahrenheit scale (F) and the Celsius scale are the temperature measurement systems that are most often used by those of us who are not scientists (C). On these scales, the reference points are the points at which steam or ice is formed, which are known as the steam point and the ice point, respectively. The freezing point is equal to 32 degrees Fahrenheit or 0 degrees Celsius. The temperature at which steam is produced is 212 degrees Fahrenheit (100 degrees Celsius). One degree Fahrenheit is equivalent to 32 degrees Celsius on the Celsius scale. Because one degree equals 1/100th of the difference between the steam and ice points, the Celsius system is simpler to use than the Fahrenheit system throughout the majority of the globe.

The Astonishing Actuality Concerning Electricity

Do you remember what your science teacher tried to explain to you back when you were in high school about how the nuclei of atoms (specifically the protons) have a positive charge while the electrons that orbit around them have a negative charge? In a typical atom, there are an equal amount of electrons and protons, which results in the atom having a neutral electrical charge. However, an atom will acquire a positive charge if it gives up one or more of its electrons to another atom, but an atom that adds an electron would have a negative charge. Electricity is a current of negatively charged particles called electrons that move along a wire at the speed of light, analogous to the way water moves through a pipe. Electrical forces occur between the charged items, and the charges on the objects that are opposite to one another "attract" (which simply means electrons want to flow from the negatively charged object to the positively charged object in order to get the objects back to their neutrally charged states). Conductors are any substances that allow an electric current to pass through them without resistance. Insulators and nonconductors are both terms that refer to substances that do not readily allow an electron current to pass through them.

In materials known as conductors, such as metal wires, the electrons have the freedom to move about, and the movement of these electrons is referred to as current. The way that the current travels from one spot to another are referred to as the circuit, and one common illustration of this is the wires. A channel that is continuously connected from a power supply to an appliance or gadget, often known as "the load," is what we mean when we talk about a circuit. Current will cease to flow if the circuit is broken in any way, including by opening a switch or blowing a fuse. This electricity is then changed into other types of energy, such as heat, light, or sound, by the appliance or gadget that is being used.

Therefore, electrical current is the movement of electrons from a region with a high electric potential (one that has an excessive number of electrons) to a region with a low electric potential (not enough electrons). This difference is what causes the flow of electricity, which is analogous to the movement of water from an area of high pressure to an area of low pressure. The potential difference, which may also be thought of as electrical pressure, is expressed in terms of volts (V).

You will most likely get familiar with the words direct current (DC) and alternating current (AC)

Off Grid Living

(DC). Direct current, or DC, refers to the unidirectional flow of electric current. Alternating current, on the other hand, will sometimes go in the other direction due to the manner it is created. Batteries and photovoltaic cells are the primary sources of direct current (DC), which is created when a fixed negative point is connected to a fixed positive point. AC is produced by generators with poles that rotate at a rate of sixty times per second, which causes the current to flow in the opposite direction. It refers to the sort of electric current that is supplied to your house by the local utility grid. By using an inverter, direct current (DC) may be changed into alternating current (AC). There are inverters available on the market that have large outputs of AC power and conversion efficiency of up to 90 percent.

The magnitude of the potential difference, measured in volts, as well as the resistance of the individual components that make up the circuit, determine the amount of current that is able to flow through it. Amperes are the units used to measure current. To some degree, the passage of current is impeded by the resistance of all substances, including conductors. This results in a lower total current. Resistance is measured using the ohm as the standard unit of measurement. A current of one ampere will flow through a resistance of one ohm when one volt is applied as "pressure." An ampere is abbreviated as "amp."

Electrical energy carried by a current is converted into different kinds of energy by components in an electrical circuit. These components may be things like lightbulbs (heat and light). Either in series or in parallel, the components of a circuit may be laid out in their configuration.

The batteries in a flashlight are arranged in a series, which raises the question of what happens to the voltage and current when the batteries are connected in this way. When components are connected in series, the voltages accumulate, but the current does not. When amps are connected in parallel, the current increases, but the voltage does not. Don't worry about it; I'll go over this topic once again in a bit when we discuss the wiring of solar panels and battery banks.

Photovoltaic Cells

A solar cell is the smallest structural unit that is capable of producing energy all by itself and is contained inside a solar panel. A cell consists of a sandwich of semiconductor materials, which are the same materials that are used in the construction of transistors. Phosphorus makes up the initial layer of the structure (an N-type or negative semiconductor). The absorber is located in the intermediate layer (P-N junction). It is composed of silicon that has been cleaned up. Boron is used to construct the third layer (a P-type or positive semiconductor). Each atom of phosphorous contains an extra atom, but each atom of boron does not have the correct number of electrons. The energy from the sun causes some of the free electrons in the phosphorous layer to be ejected, and this causes a current to desire to flow because the additional electrons are attempting to make up for the electron deficiency in the boron. The three middle layers are placed in such a manner that they are sandwiched between two electrical contact layers, which together provide a channel through which electrons may flow.

The cells are contained inside of a see-through material, such as tempered glass on the front and a protective substance on the rear of the encasing. The vast majority of panels are waterproofed, but there are some on the market that require the purchaser to add silicone sealant to the panel's frame, plugs, wire entries, and connections in order to make the panel watertight.

Off Grid Living

About a half volt is produced by each individual cell. In order to create solar panels with greater voltages, the individual cells in the panel are connected in series. Your 18-watt solar panel is presumably constructed up of 36 separate cells, each rated at 0.5 amps. The quantity of sunlight as well as the arrangement (series versus parallel) of several solar panels that make up what is known as an array influence the overall amount of current as well as the total amount of voltage that is produced. The wattage that a solar panel is capable of producing may be calculated by multiplying its rated voltage by its rated current. Solar charging systems that operate on 12, 24, or 36 volts are the standard in the market today. 12V is sufficient for demands that are less than 2 kWh. There is a good chance that a panel with a rating for a 12V system may produce an effective voltage of up to 17 volts. Larger requirements will call for either 24 or 36V. If the voltage rate of the panels produced by various manufacturers can be compared, then they may be incorporated into the system (within a volt or two).

There are primarily four ways to manufacture solar cells, which are as follows:

1. The most effective of the four different kinds of cells is the single crystalline variety, which is also the most convenient way of manufacturing. This method also results in the highest costs overall. Doping the crystal with phosphorous on one side and boron on the other is accomplished by cutting it from a thick rod of silicon and then doping it with both elements.

2. Polycrystalline silicon is likewise cut from a fat rod of a kind of silicon, but unlike single crystalline silicon, it does not go through the same cooling control process, nor does it need the same level of purity. The end product is a

matrix consisting of several different crystals. These cells are only 90 percent as effective as single crystalline cells, despite the fact that it is less expensive to construct. This is because crystal borders have a tendency to block the passage of electrons.

3. Drawing thread across liquid silicon produces thin sheets that may subsequently be doped to become string ribbon cells. These cells are produced by string ribbon cells. Although the production of these cells is inexpensive, their efficiency is only around 75% of that of single crystalline cells.

4. The production of amorphous cells, also known as thin film cells, involves vaporizing a silicon-based substance and then painting it on untempered glass or flexible stainless steel. The efficiency of these cells is comparable to that of other kinds of cells, and they are quite susceptible to shattering. These are the cells

that you find on smaller RV and boat systems. Small panels to trickle-charge your car batteries are often marketed at truck stops.

Solar cells do not include any inherent capability for storage of any kind. Wind and water turbines both have the same problem. If that is the method that you want to use to generate power, then you will be storing that electricity in a battery bank that has 12, 24, or 36 volts. Fortunately, the installation of a PV system is not too complicated. The panels themselves include no moving components and need a very low level of maintenance.

Hours of full sunshine per square meter, also known as peak sun hours, are the unit of measurement used to indicate the complete quantity of radiation energy that is accessible. This quantity, which is also referred to as the insolation value, represents the typical amount of sunlight that is received on a daily basis over the whole year. At the time, referred to as the "peak sun," the sun's rays hit the surface of the planet at a rate of 1,000 watts per square meter. One kilowatt-hour of sunlight is equal to one kilowatt per square meter, which is equivalent to one watt. Simply enter "insolation map" into the search bar of any search engine on the Internet, and you will be presented with a selection of hundreds of maps that may assist you in determining the insolation value at your location.

When measured on a cloudless day at sea level, the proportion of solar energy that solar modules are able to absorb is used to evaluate their overall performance. The quantity of solar energy that a cell will get is diminished when factors such as the weather, temperature, air pollution, altitude, season, dust, and anything covering the panel (such as snow, ice, droplets, dust, or mud) are present. At higher elevations, the efficiency of cells is at its peak. However, at the average height of the earth's surface (about 2,250 feet), clean cells will receive around 85 percent of the available radiation. Only around ten percent of it is successfully converted into electrical energy by single crystalline and polycrystalline cells; amorphous and string ribbon cells are considerably less effective in the conversion process.

Solar cells have a lifespan of many decades. A single or polycrystalline cell will lose 1% of its efficiency every two to four years, depending on whatever kind of cell it is. Solar panels need nothing in the way of upkeep and repair. Because there are no moving components, all that is required of you is to maintain them clean and prevent them from breaking.

It is possible to cause harm to a battery by charging it to its maximum capacity. When a battery has reached its maximum capacity, the current coming from the charging device — whether it's powered by the wind, the sun, or the water — should either be shut off or utilized to charge or operate another battery bank or appliance. In order to prevent the battery bank from being overcharged, a charge controller should be installed between the charging equipment and the battery pack. The controller removes the plug from the circuit, which puts a halt to the flow of power. When the controller detects that the battery's charge is once again beginning to decrease, it will open the circuit once again so that the battery bank may receive electricity from the charging device. The voltage of your battery bank and the amperage output of your panel system must be compatible with the controller you choose.

Controllers may range from very easy to very difficult to use. Their capacity is measured in terms of the amps that they are able to draw from a solar array. The procedure known as pulse-width modulation (PWM), which is used by advanced controllers, guarantees that batteries are charged effectively and will last for a long time. Even more sophisticated controllers make use of a technique known as maximum power point tracking (MPPT), which is a method that increases the number of amps that are sent into the battery while simultaneously decreasing the output voltage. According to Ohm's Law, in the event that the wattage remains the same, there must be a corresponding rise in current in the event that the voltage drops.

Low voltage disconnect (LVD) and battery temperature correction are features that are included on certain controllers (BTC). An LVD has terminals that allow for the connection of loads, which are then voltage-sensitive after they are connected. In the event that the battery voltage decreases to an unsafe level, the loads will be immediately removed. This will result in less damage being done to the batteries. Batteries are susceptible to temperature changes. The charging rate is modified by BTC depending on the current temperature.

Because of a phenomenon referred to as reverse current, it is possible for the battery to lose part of its charge throughout the night and on overcast days. Some solar panels are equipped with a diode that prevents current flow in the opposite direction. Panels that do not have their own internal diodes may have external diodes fitted to them.

When you are shopping for solar panels, be sure to pay attention to the wattage ratings. The vast majority of manufacturers only provide the rating for the best possible scenario, which takes into account full sunlight as well as ideal circumstances for elevation above sea level, temperature, and absence of clouds. Don't let this trick you in any way. Because of a variety of factors, it is not how often your panel will operate at that level. To begin, finding a spot with direct sunlight is difficult. Even in the more rural parts of the Southwest, there is often sufficient haze in the air on days when there is no cloud cover, but there is wind, which might restrict the amount of sunlight that reaches your array. At greater elevations and in more isolated places that are not impacted by pollution, cells get more sunlight.

The temperature is another thing to consider. When exposed to high temperatures, cells function less effectively. If the temperature outdoors is high enough to make you uncomfortable, it's generally too high for your array to operate at its peak efficiency. Mounting your array such that the backs of the panels have enough ventilation and making sure that the whole array is not contained in a natural or manufactured amphitheater that functions as a sun warmer is the most effective strategy to defend against this. When all of these aspects are taken into consideration, it should be evident that solar electrical systems are likely to be more effective in isolated or rural areas that are dry, high in altitude, and have a tendency to have lower temperatures and less cloud cover, and less haze.

The use of shade and shadows is the third and most significant consideration. A shadow will be cast on the panel if something is positioned between it and the sun. This will result in the panel producing less energy. A seemingly little shadow may have a domino impact on subsequent events. Imagine the array to be a bucket and the flow of sunlight to be a stream of water coming out of a faucet. Your objective is to pour water into the bucket until it is so full that it spills over. That sums up what your array is used for, basically. The battery bank receives the "overflow" of the power that it stores as it charges up. Now... let's ponder some more about the bucket. When these thirsty folks arrive, they immediately begin filling their cups straight from the stream, far in advance of the water reaching the bucket. What is the result? The bucket does have some water in it, but it does not yet have sufficient volume for it to be considered full. To put it another way, shadows and shade will do just that to your array. In an array comprised of crystalline cells, even a shadow the size of a basketball may render the whole system inoperable. There are two important lessons to be learned from this story: Mounting your array such that it is perpendicular to the sun at solar noon will ensure that it receives the most sunlight possible while also experiencing the least amount of shadow (more on this later). Second, make sure that your panels are always clean.

Off Grid Living

Solar arrays provide the most effective results when they are oriented to face the sun at a straight angle (also known as 90 degrees or perpendicular). You may as well position your array such that it is always oriented at an angle equal to your latitude, at a degree that is 90 degrees to solar noon, give or take a few degrees depending on whether it is winter or summer. Either a clinometer, which is a device that measures angles of inclination, or a swing-arm protractor may make this task quite simple.

Mounting methods hold the panels firmly in place, protecting them from being blown over by the wind while also permitting ventilation and the circulation of cool air beneath the panels. Mounts may be purchased commercially in a variety of configurations, including ground or roof mounts, pole mounts, and flush mounts, among others. When making homemade mounts, corrosion-resistant materials like anodized aluminum or galvanized steel should be used wherever possible. Wood is OK, but it won't endure as long as other materials. Slotted steel angle stock is simple to work with and widely accessible in most hardware stores. Be certain that there is not a single portion of your mount that will cause a shadow to fall on the panel. It is common practice to deploy portable arrays on wide-base A-frame ladders or stepladder platforms.

Adjustable tilt is useful for making seasonal changes to the angle of the panel, but tracking devices that follow the sun across the sky are not only costly but also not as successful as you would hope they would be. It would be more beneficial to spend the money on purchasing more panels and batteries. (The appendices at the back of the book have further information on other mounting techniques; feel free to check them out.)

In conclusion, solar electricity is quite effective for most home appliances, with the exception of those that are very big and use many huge electric heating elements (water heater, clothes dryer, electric stove, electric heater, etc.). Consider utilizing propane, natural gas, or another option to power these items in order to reduce the size of the solar system that you'll need to support their operation.

Wind Systems

Wind power is often used in order to move an item from one point to another or to rotate an appliance around an axis. Sailboats and wind turbines are two typical examples of devices that may produce power. Since sailing is not the subject of this book, we will focus on the turbines instead. When the wind blows through a wind turbine, it rotates a rotor blade assembly, which in turn spins a shaft. The shaft is linked to an alternator or generator that generates power by using the rotation of the shaft.

Horizontal-axis turbines, which resemble a propeller and have two or three blades (rotors), and vertical-axis turbines, which are sometimes referred to as "eggbeater" turbines, are the two most popular types of wind turbines. Horizontal-axis turbines may be used to generate electricity. Upwind turbines are distinguished from downwind turbines by their orientation relative to the wind. The blades of upwind turbines, like those of the vast majority of three-blade horizontal-axis turbines, are oriented such that they face the direction of the wind while the turbine is being run. Horizontal-axis turbines with bigger rotor diameters capture more wind and produce more energy than those with smaller rotor diameters because there is a greater surface area exposed to the wind. If a residence is anything between average and big in size, it will most likely need a turbine with a rotor radius of at least 5 feet and a total wingspan of 10 feet in order to produce enough power to be completely independent of the grid. These smaller turbines, also known as mini-turbines, have rotor radii that range from 2.5 to 5 feet and are ideal for use in holiday cottages and residences with a smaller footprint. Micro-turbines, which have rotor radii ranging from 1.5 to 2.5 feet, may be used in transient and recreational settings (boats, RVs, etc.).

Sizing Your System

Before deciding how large of a system you need, you must first ascertain the total number of watts that will be used and the total period of time that those watts will be utilized (watt-hours). After that, you may contrast those numbers with the number of accessible energy resources (sun, wind, water head, and flow, available at your geographic location). Utilize this information to calculate the size of the components, as well as the number of them that will be required to provide the quantity of power that you demand.

In conclusion, I'd want to restate something that should be obvious: the size of your system may be significantly decreased by using a few conservation strategies. Make use of energy-saving lights and home equipment, and think about finding alternatives to using electricity.

Batteries Every stand-alone system and utility interface system has to have batteries, either individual batteries or battery banks. Nickel-cadmium (NiCad) and lead-acid (L-A) batteries are the two kinds of rechargeable batteries that are used the most often nowadays. Batteries that use lead acid contain plates made of lead that are soaked in sulfuric acid. Plates of nickel and cadmium that are immersed in a potassium hydroxide solution are found in NiCad batteries.

The least expensive and most widely accessible kind of battery is lead-acid. When looking for L-A batteries, the depth of the charging cycle should be your first concern. These batteries come in a variety of shapes and sizes, but that is not the most significant consideration.

Batteries designed for shallow cycling, like those seen in cars, produce high currents for only brief durations. As a result of their inability to withstand repeated deep discharging (below 20 percent), they are not appropriate for use in PV systems.

Batteries that fall into the deep-cycle category are designed to withstand repeated discharges of up to 80 percent of their total capacity. In spite of this, if you cycle these batteries less deeply, they will last far longer. Make every effort to maintain a capacity greater than 50 percent. If the L-A batteries are not recharged after each cycle, they will all fail much sooner than expected. Sulfation of the positive plate and irreversible loss of capacity may occur in an L-A battery that has been drained for a lengthy period of time. It is possible to increase the battery's lifespan by installing an electrical desulfated.

Although nickel-cadmium batteries are more costly, they have a lifespan that is many times greater than that of L-A batteries. NiCads can be discharged to the extent of one hundred percent and can continue to be discharged without suffering any loss of capability. In addition, their capability does not decrease when exposed to cold temperatures, and freezing does not harm them in any way. From fully charged to completely discharged, there is no change in voltage. Because of these reasons, it is possible to utilize batteries with a lesser capacity.

NiCad batteries have the same efficiency when it comes to charging as L-A batteries, and their rate of self-discharge is quite low. When compared to L-A batteries, they need a voltage that is between 16 and 17 volts in order to be fully charged. This is for a 12-volt battery. The greater voltage is something that most AC battery chargers are unable to supply, but certain solar panels can. Take note that certain inverters rated for 12 volts may momentarily turn off if connected to a battery with that voltage.

The bank is always open for deposits of more NiCads at any moment. L-A banks will "dumb down" to match the battery that has the lowest capacity or is the least efficient among them.

The charge and discharge voltages, overall life, and performance at low temperatures of nickel-iron batteries are comparable to those of nickel-cadmium batteries. On the other hand, they do not provide the high amperage that NiCads provide, which means that a bigger battery will be required to produce the same amount of power. The fact that these batteries are made without lead or cadmium is yet another advantage of purchasing them.

A typical L-A battery comprises cells that are not hermetically sealed and which house liquid acid.

They may develop leaks. Batteries known by the terms gel-cell, AGM, and sealed lead acid are examples of alternatives to the conventional lead acid variety. Gel-cell and AGM batteries, in particular, have advantages over their traditional L-A counterparts.

Gel cells make use of acid in a semisolid gel form, making them less likely to leak than traditional cells. One potential drawback is that a coating may build on the battery plates, which would decrease their level of performance.

Batteries that employ something called an absorbent glass mat, or AGM, have glass mats on the inside that soak up the acid. Although there is a slightly increased risk of leakage due to cracks in AGM batteries compared to gel-cell batteries, AGMs provide a more consistent level of performance.

Any battery that employs lead acid as its electrolyte and is hermetically sealed is considered to be a sealed lead-acid battery. This covers AGM batteries as well as gel-cell batteries. The battery fluid in sealed batteries does not need to be refilled, which is one of the many apparent benefits of using these types of batteries. There is also a reduced risk of leakage. They need very little upkeep if any at all.

The needed amount of storage space, the maximum discharge rate, and the lowest temperature at the location of the battery bank are the factors that decide the size of the battery bank (for L-A batteries). L-A batteries can only perform at 75 percent of their capacity when the temperature is 40 degrees Fahrenheit, and they can only function at 50 percent when the temperature is 0 degrees Fahrenheit.

The amount of storage that a device has is measured in amp-hours. The capacity of the battery bank measured in amp-hours should be sufficient to ensure that the required amount of power can be delivered even if the sky remains overcast for an extended length of time. To this, you must add an additional 20 percent for L-A batteries. The size of the battery bank may be reduced if there is also a secondary source of power, such as a generator that also serves as a battery charger.

Controllers of Electrical Charge

Let's review the most important things we've learned about charge controllers: When a battery has reached its maximum capacity, the electricity that is being supplied by the charging device should be either cut off or diverted to charge or power another battery bank or appliance. In order to prevent the battery bank from being overcharged, a charge controller should be installed between the charging equipment and the battery pack. The controller removes the plug from the circuit, which puts a halt to the flow of power. When the controller detects that the battery's charge is once again beginning to decrease, it will open the circuit once again so that the battery bank may receive electricity from the charging device. Both the voltage of the battery bank and the amperage of the charging device system have to be compatible with the controller in order for it to work properly.

The number of amps that a controller is able to handle from a solar array is how it is rated. The procedure known as pulse-width modulation (PWM), which is used by advanced controllers, guarantees that batteries are charged effectively and will last for a long time. Maximum power point tracking, often known as MPPT, is a method that increases the number of amps that are fed into the battery while simultaneously decreasing the output voltage of the controller.

A low voltage disconnect LVD makes it possible to attach loads to its terminals, which are then voltage-sensitive once the connection has been made. In the event that the battery voltage decreases to an unsafe level, the loads will be immediately removed. This will result in less damage being done to the batteries. Batteries are susceptible to temperature changes. Battery temperature compensation, often known as BTC, modifies the charging rate according to the temperature of the battery.

Charge controllers with extra features and functionality are referred to as "monitor" or "regulator" devices. In most cases, they will come equipped with an ammeter for measuring the current, voltage set points that may be adjusted, and LED lights to indicate the charge state.

Inverters

Through a process that involves transforming, filtering, and stepping voltages, inverters are able to change the DC that is stored in batteries into AC on demand (changing them from one level to

Off Grid Living

another). The output is going to be cleaner if there is more processing done, but this is going to come at the sacrifice of the efficiency of the conversion.

Housing

Convenience is the primary consideration for most off-gridders when selecting the property on which to build their houses, which is an unusual phenomenon considering the multitude of reasons that people have for wanting to live off the grid. How far away is the Wal-Mart that's the closest to me? Where is the closest hospital? Which is closer, the high school or the college? People who say they live off the grid but whose choices are mostly driven by considerations of their own comfort and convenience are, in a way, nonetheless hopelessly connected to the grid.

The following are some of the other criteria that off-gridders consider important while looking for the ideal location for their homes:

1. Good access to sunlight, with slopes that face south for the purpose of passive heating and earth sheltering. When building a shelter into the slope

of the soil, a technique known as "earth sheltering," you require a portion of the land to have a decent slope angle.

2. Complete and unrestricted exposure to the wind.
3. Arid land that is well-drained and has stable soils, in addition to land that has an adequate supply of water
4. A climate that is favorable for year-round comfort and a microclimate, as well as excellent topsoil that is beneficial to the growth of food and provides shade and shelter from the wind.
5. Resources located on-site for construction (trees, rocks, sand, clay, etc.).
6. The growth of off-grid systems must face no legal obstacles, or at least very few.
7. Good views.
8. No pollution.

Off Grid Living

Finding the location, drawing a map of it, choosing a home design, and drafting comprehensive plans for it are the primary phases in the process of putting together your site. The last step is the actual building (or purchase) of the shelter.

There are undoubtedly millions of individuals who might need some financial relief from their monthly power costs and who, with the right kind of assistance, could convert what they currently have into an off-grid dwelling. The vast majority of individuals just do not have the financial resources to be able to go out and purchase a plot of land, get an architect and construction crew to design and build their off-grid ideal home, and then proceed to live happily ever after. Let's tone it down a bit and be more practical about it. We may make a humble beginning by instituting some energy-saving practices that will bring our monthly power costs down, and then we can gradually increase those efforts.

Off Grid Living

The several fundamental locations that are accessible for an off-grid living might be used to make a determination on the necessary shelter.

5. The first kind of housing is known as the transitory venue. This category includes lifestyles that are oriented toward mobile habitations (such as RVs), transient dwellings (tents, hogans, and huts), and habitations that have a footprint that is smaller than 250 square feet.

6. The second kind of venue is known as the intermittent venue, and it consists of fixed or mobile habitations (cabins, bigger motor homes, and trailers) that have a footprint ranging from 250 to 750 square feet. These habitations may be occupied intermittently or permanently.

7. The third kind of venue is referred to as the permanent venue, and it consists of fixed habitations that have a footprint that is more

than 750 square feet. These are the residences of people who fall into the middle class and above in the United States.

Let's take some time to look at passive solar architecture before we go on to discuss the specifics of the shelters in each of the three locations. Even in houses that were not constructed with the intention of making use of solar energy, it is possible to make low-cost adjustments to increase a home's energy efficiency by using the principles of passive solar architecture.

Construction Using Only the Sun's Energy

A way of heating and lighting a place with the minimum amount of input from the grid is referred to as passive solar design. The following is a list of the most important pieces of the solar design puzzle:

- Components

Windows that face due south. These should enable the sun to penetrate at a low angle throughout the winter months. The heat from the sunshine is then stored in a thermal mass once it has been transformed.

Thermodynamic mass. Brick, stone, concrete, drywall, tile, and earthen materials are all examples of this kind of heat-absorbing material that may be found in walls (sometimes referred to as Trombe walls), floors, and ceilings. In order to fulfill its purpose, thermal mass must first transform the sun's rays into heat, then radiate that heat, and finally, store any extra heat for later use (to keep you warm all night long).

- Overhangs. Overhangs control solar gain. As is well knowledge, the sun's position in relation to the earth changes with time. It is at its highest point in the summer and at its lowest point in the winter. The overhangs, also known as the eaves, provide shade to the windows and walls of the home, so limiting the amount of direct sunlight that enters the structure during the warmer months. During the winter, when the sun's angle is lower, more sunlight penetrates buildings, which results in an increase in the amount of heat produced.

- Insulation as well as covers for the windows. These should create a coating that is continuous all the way through the walls, ceiling, and foundation, as well as over the windows and skylights. During the colder months, this insulating layer will keep the warmth inside, and during the warmer months, it will keep the heat outside.
- Ventilation. Essential for achieving a uniform distribution of the warm or cold air.

In the dead of winter, how much heat can the sun produce? These blinds melted under the heat that was created in that area by the combination of direct sunshine and the light that was reflected off of the snow. They were sandwiched between a glass window and a thin layer of plastic sheeting. That afternoon, the average temperature in the surrounding air was 24 degrees.

Solar power may be integrated into the architecture of a house in a variety of different ways. The easiest designs are sun-tempered, which is a word that indicates the design makes use of the most straightforward approaches to gathering the sun's energy. Sun-tempered designs are the simplest designs. For instance, solar heat collection will be maximized when the long axis of the home runs east-west when there are numerous windows or only a few extremely big windows along the south side of the house; and when the structure is well insulated and maybe has thermal mass added to it.

Off Grid Living

A real solar design incorporates an even greater window area on the south side, in addition to an increased amount of insulation and thermal mass. This building retains a significant amount of the sun's direct heat gain, which is obtained via the windows and transferred into the thermal mass. The attached sunrooms are able to gather heat via the windows that face the south side of the building. This heat may then be transferred into the home through convection—with the assistance of tiny fans—through doors, windows, or vents. This kind of passive solar energy is called isolated-gain passive solar. The genuine solar structure will be outfitted with an efficient thermal mass, also known as a Trombe wall. Trombe walls are often constructed out of the earth, brick, or cement and are typically painted black.

When attempting to solarize a house, there are a variety of other considerations to take into account. The general rule of thumb is to make things as straightforward and manageable as possible. Take note of the following considerations that are essential:

➤ It is more difficult to heat large buildings than it is to heat smaller ones. The longer side of the construction may be oriented to face the sun if it is oriented along an east-west axis that is 90 degrees to true south. That should be the location of the large windows. In the winter, heat may be lost via windows that face north and east, and in the summer, windows that face west can cause the inside to become too hot. Thus these types of windows should be minimized and kept to a minimum. (To prevent the inside from being too heated by the sun during the summer, install overhangs over the windows. In most cases, an overhang of two feet is sufficient.)

➤ If it is at all practicable, you should dig into a slope that faces south and construct the building such that the north side is hidden in the berm. This technique is known as earth sheltering.

- The thermal mass found within the building stores heat during the winter and remains relatively cold during the summer; this contributes to the building not overheating. To ensure that the thermal mass heats the whole building, it should be distributed evenly throughout the interior. Narrow rectangular masses enable heat to many rooms independently without the need for fans or ducts. Additionally, they assist in blocking the sun from the inner surface of the east and west walls.

- Be sure to insulate the building. Insulation levels should be increased above what is needed by the code. Insulation should be protected from moisture since exposure to moisture lowers its thermal resistance.

Insulation made of cellulose and fiberglass is particularly susceptible to damage from it. The installation of vapor barriers on walls may be of some assistance; nevertheless, the most common entry points for moisture are penetrations such as loose fittings around doors, windows, and roofs, as well as via tiny holes in the walls. Be careful to caulk and flash these penetrations as thoroughly as possible.

➢ It is important that batt insulation not be squeezed and that it be installed flat against the structure. Products made of liquid foam provide a watertight barrier and block the passage of air. It is essential to have insulated windows on the east, north, and west-facing walls of the building. When night falls, make sure that the windows are covered with insulated shades or hard thermal shutters.

➢ Take into consideration installing radiation barriers on the roof. It is essential to have enough ventilation on the inside in order to distribute the heat properly.

- Construct buildings with an airtightness level that is as high as you can get it. In the winter, sealing penetrations prevents the entry of cold air and the exfiltration of heat, while in the summer, sealing penetrations prevents the infiltration of warm air and the exfiltration of cold air. When the doorway to the primary building is opened, a sealed entrance, which is sometimes referred to as an airlock, stops air from flowing in and out of the building. Earth sheltering not only decreases infiltration and egress but also lessens the amount of heat that is lost via the building's outer walls and roof. In addition to this, it wraps the structure in a thermal blanket, which helps to keep the building toasty in the winter and refreshingly cool in the summer.

- Maintain certain portions of the building that are shaded from the sun. They will provide some relief if it gets to be too hot to bear.
- Maintain a secondary source of heat in the form of a wood burner, electric space heater with low wattage, or heater that runs on propane.

Transient Shelters

Let's not equate the austerity of this location with that of living on the street. This is not a discussion about hiding out in freight cars or sleeping in cardboard boxes. These are houses and other buildings that may be inhabited, and there are really more of them out there than you would imagine there would be.

Tents and other forms of soft shelter

Nomadic people have been known to make use of tents from a time that predates the recording of historical events. One such structure is the tepee, which was used by a number of Native American tribes. There are still many people who choose to live in traditional dwellings such as tents, such as the Bedouins of the Arabian Peninsula. Behind enemy lines, contemporary militaries often set up their headquarters in tents. When traveling into the wilderness for recreational or exploratory reasons, they are an essential piece of equipment that should be brought along by both people and groups. In the event of a natural catastrophe, they may also serve as temporary homes and storage areas. Tents are a viable option for self-sufficient living or vacationing on a budget when the temperature is temperate, the latitude is low, and there is a presence of marine currents that create an environment that is continuously pleasant.

Ruins belonging to the Anasazi people that can be found in the southeast corner of Utah suggest that they had a good understanding of passive solar heating and cooling a thousand years ago.

Tents have three major selling points: first, they are inexpensive; second, they are portable; and third, they are easy to set up and can be done so in a short amount of time.

Tents may be constructed out of a wide variety of materials; however, nylon and cotton canvas is the most typical choices. Nylon is the material of choice in modern times owing to the fact that it is both lightweight and unable to absorb substantial amounts of moisture. Coatings of silicon and polyurethane, among other chemicals, are often applied to nylon materials in order to render them almost impervious to water. The propensity of nylon to degrade when exposed to UV rays is one of the material's drawbacks (i.e., sunlight). A tent that is only occupied at certain times of the year may persist for many seasons, but a permanent home made of nylon would be lucky to last a single year when exposed to the sun. Even if you have to change a tent annually, it is still a better value than purchasing a "hard shelter" due to the lower cost of tents in comparison to those of permanent structures. Cotton canvas is dense and has a high capacity for absorbing moisture (making it even heavier). When it takes in water, the threads expand and become more closely packed, which finally causes the tent to become incredibly water-resistant for a short period of time.

Tents may be found in a wide variety of styles and sizes. The vast majority of the tents that are sold are dome tents that are held up by poles that are attached to the outside. You should look for a tent that has poles and/or fly (rain coverings) that are shock-corded to the main structure. These are some of the extra elements that you should look for. The construction of the item with two walls not only makes it heavier but also makes it more durable and resistant to the elements. It's good to have doors and windows that have bug screens. A further advantage is the presence of dual zippers on the doors and windows.

Because we are now discussing zippers, I should warn you that the zippers on a cheap tent will be the first item to break, and they can almost never be fixed. This will leave you with a tent that has doors and windows that won't shut properly. If you purchase an inexpensive tent, as soon as you bring it home, inspect the zippers and clip away any loose threads or material that might get stuck in the zipper. This is especially important if you bought the tent online. Your stake loops and the fabric channels that link the tent to the frame are going to be the next items on your inexpensive tent to give out to you. These are not successful since the cloth is of low quality and there is insufficient stitching. If you plan on purchasing an inexpensive tent, you might think about using your own sewing machine to double or even triple stitch any of the seams or channels that will be subjected to significant amounts of strain. By stitching a patch onto a vulnerable spot, you might potentially prevent it from ripping by spreading the strain across a larger area and spreading it out more evenly.

The question is, what exactly is a "cheap tent"? Let's just say that if you're buying floor space for less than one dollar per square foot, you're probably investing in something that won't last very long. Although this is not always the case, in most situations, it is accurate. Purchase well-known brand names that you know you can rely on. When selecting a tent to use as a house, the following are some extra considerations to take into account:

The Living Space

You want there to be enough space for you, your roommates, and all of your belongings. It is

Off Grid Living

recommended that you have at least sixty square feet of floor space per individual in order to avoid experiencing feelings of claustrophobia. If you want to be able to accommodate a few visitors on occasion, you should really consider doubling the size. If you add some space for a few extra amenities (such as a table and chairs), you'll have enough room (120 square feet minimum). If you're not going to be doing any cooking outdoors or in a separate tent, you'll need an additional 40 square feet for your kitchen. We've expanded to a total of 160 square feet.

Is it true that they create tents as large as that? Yes. Use the Eureka Copper Canyon 1610 as your transportation. This tent is designed in the manner of a cabin and has vertical walls. It has a bedroom that is 80 square feet and a screened-in lounge that is also 80 square feet. Because the screens feature storm coverings that pull back, the whole tent may be kept dry even when there is a storm outside. It is equipped with a connection for extension cords as well as a multitude of loops for hanging lights. In addition to that, it has a ceiling height of seven feet. If you want to truly transform a tent into a house, the ceiling height and the amount of head space are critical considerations. A major disappointment is when you get to your own house, and you can't even stand up straight there. This tent is priced at $2 per square foot to purchase.

Is there anything that can compare in size? Yes. Consider, as still another example, the Eureka Condo, which is a three-room cabin tent measuring 10 1/2 by 20 feet and including abundant head space. It costs around $3.80 per square foot to purchase.

Durability

You should look for a tent that has substantial, sturdy poles that will prevent the structure from collapsing or laying flat when subjected to the force of light to moderate blizzard. The seams have to be double-stitched and sealed, and there ought to be heavy-duty zippers on both the windows and the doors. A tent that may be used in spring, summer, and autumn is called a "three-season tent." These tents are ideal for usage in locations with milder four seasons. As long as the poles are solid and appropriately fastened, the tent is anchored, all of the guy lines are staked, and the fly and guy lines are tensioned correctly, they work well in windy circumstances. When compared to what is known as four-season or adventure tents, three-season tents contain fewer poles, are made of lighter fabrics and have designs that are less aerodynamic. Investing in a quality tent that can be used in all four seasons is money well spent.

Defense against the effects of water

Many cheaply produced tents do not come with a rain flap and instead put all of their faith in the fact that the material they are composed of is waterproof. Steer clear of them. Condensation will form on waterproof ceilings as a result of breathing and cooking, and it will either flow down onto the floor or onto the people living there. On the other side, there are some pricey tents that are created from a material that is both breathable and a vapor barrier. These tents are able to deflect rain and reduce condensation. Invest in a tent that comes equipped with a rain flap just to be safe. "Double-walled tents" is the term used to describe camping shelters that come equipped with a rain flap. The fly should cover the majority of the tent, including any windows or skylights that cannot be zipped shut, and it should also cover the majority of the tent. Look for a tent that has a fly that can be adjusted for tightness and that is shock-corded (the tie downs or stake loops are elasticized). A vestibule is an extension of the tent that does not have the floor. There is a zipper that may be used to entirely separate the vestibule from the sleeping section of the tent. Because of this, vestibules are the perfect places to change out of soiled clothing and kick off filthy shoes before entering the main tent.

Protection against Insects

Bug screens must be installed in each and every entrance, including air vents, doors, and windows. Use duct tape to cover any openings in your home that are not protected by screening if you live in an area that is plagued by persistent infestations of especially unpleasant pests, such as centipedes or scorpions (e.g., the utility port).

There are a great number of reputable tent manufacturers that develop and sell tents of a size and quality that are comparable to one another. Examine the online customer reviews of the tent to get a sense of its level of craftsmanship. Before you purchase a tent, it is a good idea to check it out in person at the sporting goods shop near your home.

Yurts

Yurt is a term that has been westernized from its original Asian form and refers to the traditional spherical houses that nomadic peoples make use of. When people in places like Europe and North America hear the term, their minds automatically go to the more contemporary forms. In European countries, these tents are typically made of canvas and have trellis walls. In North America, the term "yurt" can refer to a number of different types of round wooden-framed homes, such as tapered-wall and frame-panel yurts, or it can refer to a round portable home known as a fabric yurt. There are several situations in which the differences between a yurt and a tent or cabin tent are almost indistinguishable.

Yurts are traditionally constructed with a cluster of roof poles that are joined to a central ring. As gravity pulls down the heavy center-ring joints, the roof poles are pushed outward into the perimeter, thereby creating a ceiling that does not require any internal supports such as posts or center poles. The roof poles' far ends are embedded in a fortified top-of-the-wall perimeter, and as gravity pulls down the heavy center-ring joints, the roof poles are pushed outward into the perimeter. Only the walls themselves need support, which is given by the framework in the form of a circular trellis. The steepness of the roof combined with the rounded form creates a barrier against the wind and efficiently sheds snow and rain.

What sets a yurt different from a large tent or a cabin tent, and how does it compare to these other types of tents? One thing to note is that yurts are typically set up on a platform made of wood. There are a wide variety of alternative materials that may be used as a base. Even corn cobs have been used (a mixture of sand, clay, water, and straw). A yurt can be pitched on the ground in its entirety if the climate is dry and desert-like. It is possible to dig a rock-filled trench around the base of the yurt in order to enhance the drainage.

The amount of time and money necessary to create a yurt are two more characteristics that set it apart from a tent. Although it is feasible to purchase the designs and materials for a modest yurt for as low as $3,000, yurts constructed using high-tech materials will have an average price tag of more than $15,000 when they are completed.

Tents may be erected in a hurry in just a few short minutes. The assembly time for even the largest commercial event tents is often no more than a few hours. Yurts, on the other hand, can take anywhere from a few days to several weeks. Despite having their roots in nomadic culture, yurts are just far more difficult to transport than tents. In addition, construction rules are not friendly to structures that may be categorized as temporary, such as yurts, tents, or any other similar structure. They are often seen as unhealthful eyesores that signify a step backward by local governments as well as neighbors who are pretentious. The majority of the time, in order to be in compliance with the code, you will need to have at least running water and flushing toilets.

Traditional Homes of the Indigenous Peoples of the United States

Numerous updated interpretations of traditional Native American homes are already in widespread usage; some of them may be built in a simple and cost-effective manner.

The tepee is the Native American house that is arguably the most well-known to people today. A structure in the form of a cone made of long wooden poles is erected in order to construct a tepee. First, three or four primary poles are anchored in the ground and then attached to one another towards the top. After that, more poles are added to make a roughly circular base for the structure. A watertight cover, historically fashioned from animal skins but now more often constructed from canvas, nylon, or even plastic, is pulled over the frame. Traditionally, the cover was made from animal hides. The smoke from the central fire or stove might escape via a hole at the top of the structure. This aperture may be adjusted using the cover's outside flaps, and it can be closed when the weather is stormy or damp. The cover of the tepee may be rolled up for ventilation during the warmer months of the year, even if the bottom borders of the cover are held in place by stones or pegs. In areas with colder weather, it is common practice to install an interior layer of insulation. There are tepee kits available for as little as $1,500 that have

Off Grid Living

a circumference of 25 feet. When one considers the similarities between a yurt and a commercial tepee, it is puzzling why the former is sold at a far lower price than the latter.

The traditional Navajo (Diné) dwelling is a hogan, which is a round or polygonal (six-sided or eight-sided) domed structure built of logs or poles and plastered with mud or earth. Hogans may be circular or polygonal (six-sided or eight-sided). The front door has historically been positioned such that it faces east in order to welcome the dawn. It is meant for a single household and has one huge chamber that is up to 25 feet in diameter. The Navajo were known to reside in small communities composed of numerous connected families, and each of these households had its own hogan. Around the Four Corners region, which includes Colorado, New Mexico, Utah, and Arizona, hogans are still often used.

The Pueblo Indians constructed their homes in characteristic apartment-style structures out of stone or adobe bricks (made from sun-baked clay and straw), with wooden beams serving as the primary structural element. Even though they are hundreds of years old, several of these homes are still occupied today. The ruins of ancient cultures such as the Anasazi and the Fremont can be found all over the southwestern United States. These people built their communities on the sides of cliffs and beneath rock overhangs to take advantage of passive solar energy and create a more comfortable environment in an otherwise harsh environment.

Vehicles for Pleasure or Recreation (RVs)

In spite of the fact that some people argue that the two terms refer to different things, a recreational vehicle (RV) is a wheeled or motorized enclosed

Off Grid Living

platform that serves the dual purpose of being a vehicle and a house. They provide more mobility and protection than a tent or tepee, and for the same price, they provide about the same amount of living space and comfort as a yurt. Sadly, there are a lot of recreational vehicles available today that have a nice appearance but are incapable of withstanding any level of rigorous use. Check with consumer advocacy groups and invest in a recreational vehicle that can be used for living in as well as going on vacation.

Waste Management

The majority of this chapter is devoted to a discussion on how to properly manage human waste when living off the grid. However, sewage is not the only challenge you face in terms of waste management. Waste of any form has to be handled, and for those who desire to live off the grid, there are some easy answers to some of your waste problems. However, these solutions do not address all of your waste problems. The most important aspect of waste management is reducing the amount of garbage that is produced. It does not imply that you should purchase or consume less, but rather that you should squander less. Reuse those bags, receptacles, and containers, as well as any other goods that may be used again, such as any other items that can be reused. Recyclers may make a difference by helping the environment. Composting a significant portion of one's solid waste is another option for those who live off the grid.

Recycling

Recycling refers to the process of reusing old materials to create new items. The procedure begins with the collecting of recyclables, continues with the processing of the materials, and ends with the production of the product. Glass, aluminum cans, steel, and other scrap metals, plastic bottles, paper, used motor oil, and old car batteries are just some of the materials that can be recycled. Other recyclable materials include: It's possible that the steps involved in collecting and processing each material will be very different from one another.

Recycling can also be done through the process of composting. The process takes place whenever organic waste is subjected to microbial processes in order to decompose. The term "mulching" refers to the process that takes place on the ground of a forest, and the term "mulch" refers to the final product. Composting is the name given to the process that occurs when it is carried out on purpose by humans, and the end result is also called compost. The substance that is produced can be put to use as fertilizer.

Composting necessitates the presence of water, air, and decaying matter with an appropriate ratio of nitrogen to carbon. A composting chamber needs to be tough, have holes for air circulation, and have a cover to prevent rain from getting in. Some of the containers used for composting are fixed on an axle so that they may be rotated while the contents are being mixed. Other containers may be rolled on the ground, or one may use a shovel to mix the contents of the container when it is empty.

The correct materials need to be sorted through carefully and then mixed together for the composting process to be effective. To be successful, compost requires a steady supply of nitrogen-rich vegetable waste, sometimes known as "greens." This kind of trash comes from the kitchen and also includes grass and weed clippings. It requires a roughly equal supply of carbon-rich materials, which are referred to as browns. These resources include hay, bark, wood chips, dried leaves, shredded paper or cardboard, and shredded paper.

Sewage

Gray water and black water are the two components that make up domestic wastewater. Gray water is the wastewater that is produced by activities like doing the laundry, washing dishes in the bathroom, cooking in the kitchen, and using machines that do not contain excrement. Black water typically originates from the toilet and is referred to as sewage most of the time. Gray water is not nearly as pathogenic as black water, which is full of harmful organisms. Before it can be used again, water that has been contaminated with black must be cleaned and sanitized. Even though gray water contains germs and contaminants, it is still possible to reuse it to irrigate plants and landscapes as long as certain safeguards are taken. In certain areas, the definition of "black water" includes gray water from certain sources. This is the case in states where the health departments define gray water. Gray water is often considered to be cleaner than black water, despite the fact that it is dirtier than tap water. Gray water that has been filtered may be used most effectively for the subsurface watering of landscaping plants that are not edible.

Gray-water systems may range from being simple and inexpensive to be quite complicated and pricey. Two concepts are the foundation of any gray-water system: To begin, wholesome topsoil has the ability to disinfect or filter used water. Second, it is important to note that people are unable to consume, cook with, or bathe in gray water until it has been cleaned. It is a widespread practice to drain gray water or dump it straight from buckets onto vegetation that is located outdoors; nevertheless, doing so is against the law in the majority of states. In order to eliminate contaminants and pathogens from gray water prior to its disposal, sophisticated systems purify the water using in-line filters, settling tanks, and sand filters. This is done so that the water may then be distributed via a drip system.

The design of your gray-water system will be determined by the location of the system, the climate there, the available budget, the amount of gray water you already have, the amount of irrigation you require, the permeability of the soil, the amount of work you are willing to put in, and the local health and building codes. In most cases, health officials actively discourage the use of gray-water systems. Keep in mind that water that is routed through pipes in order to pull warm water is not considered gray water and does not need treatment. Allow it to collect in a container, and then use that container to water the food plants in your garden.

The majority of individuals will find that a septic system provides them with the most convenient means of dealing with gray water. When a house is being built from scratch, it is simple and inexpensive to install black-water and gray-water systems that are distinct from one another; however, retrofitting an existing house to handle separate systems is complex and costly.

sewage treatment plants

Let's begin with the most important aspect of this situation: Installing a septic system is your best bet if you really want an off-grid approach to waste management for black- and gray-water waste without getting into a fight with the local HD and

Off Grid Living

without having to deal with the upkeep that is necessary to work with compost toilets and other similar items. You would be extremely smart to engage an experienced septic system specialist to assist you, or to build your septic system for you, just as you would be sensible to do with the majority of the off-grid preparations we've discussed in this book.

Septic systems consist of big tanks that are originally filled with water and are used to collect and dispose of wastewater. These tanks are called septic tanks. The bacteria in the tank break everything down and split the mess into three layers: a top scum layer consisting of grease, oil, and lighter fluids; a middle liquid layer called effluent; and a bottom sludge layer consisting of heavy particles. The middle liquid layer is called effluent.

The effluent that is contained inside the tank is discharged onto a drain field whenever additional wastewater is added. The pathogens are buried by the silt in the drain field, where it functions as a filter, keeping them there until the nutrients in the soil can absorb them. At the same time, anaerobic bacteria and other beneficial microorganisms are feeding on the solids that are present in the sludge and the scum. This causes the solids to be broken down, which results in the production of carbon dioxide and hydrogen sulfide gases, which are then released through the vent stack.

At the very least once every three years, and ideally once every year, a professional should pump out the contents of a septic tank and perform any necessary maintenance on it. The sediments and scum that have accumulated over time have the potential to one day fill the tank, block the system, and pollute the drain field.

That's the very best there has to offer. Now let's examine the absolute bottom of the line as well as everything that falls in between. The knowledge that is going to be provided to you here will make your neighborhood HD very happy.

Toilets that Compost Waste

A composting toilet is a container that is heated, has enough ventilation, and contains a variety of bacteria that break down waste and produce a compost that is dry, fluffy, and odorless. This is accomplished by a process known as fast aerobic decomposition, which is the antithesis of the stinky anaerobic processes that occur in outhouses. More than ninety percent of the material that is added to the compost is lost up the vent as either gas or vaporized water. The presence of unpleasant odors in a composting toilet indicates the presence of pockets of anaerobic activity brought on by poor mixing. When temperatures drop below 50 degrees Fahrenheit, the microorganisms that are responsible for composting stop functioning or go dormant.

Composting toilets include the following components:

- a place to sit,
- a composting chamber, and
- an evaporation tray is an element that is required.

These components may either be assembled into a single device or shown separately as individual components.

In order for the composting process to be successful, the space must be moist. The toilet is designed to evaporate any excess water, and any overflow may be plugged directly into a septic system. Every composting toilet is equipped with a horizontal vent pipe that allows excess moisture to escape. The evaporation tray is being crossed by the flow of air as it ascends the vent. The heat generated by the composting acts as fuel for the updraft. Composters that are powered by electricity often come equipped with ventilation fans and modest heating components to facilitate the composting process. Even the smallest composters often come equipped with some kind of mixing mechanism to guarantee that oxygen is distributed evenly throughout the pile.

Moldering is a kind of decomposition that occurs at low temperatures and is used by simple composters. They feature air passages and vents that are operated by fans, but they do not have any extra heat or mixing capabilities. Urine and water are often restricted, if not prohibited entirely. It is necessary to either manually remove liquids or pump them out. The process of mold growth might take years, during which time there is an elevated risk of pathogen survival.

There are a variety of composting toilets available for purchase, and if you search the term "do-it-yourself composting toilet" on the internet, you'll find a wealth of information pertaining to the construction of a composting toilet in your own house.

Maintaining the Contentment of Your Composter

Your composting toilet will function more effectively with anything that raises the temperature or improves the amount of airflow in the room. It is best not to use a composter in close proximity to other equipment that needs oxygen, such as a wood burner. If the composter does not get the necessary amount of oxygen, the mixture will become putrid. Insulate the vent whenever it goes through a cold region to prevent condensation from running back down the vent as it goes through the cold space. To avoid pockets of anaerobic bacteria, add one cup of a carbonaceous bulking agent (like peat or wood chips) every couple of days. This will allow the extra moisture to be absorbed while also producing air gaps that will keep the pockets from becoming anaerobic.

Primitive Methods of Waste Disposal

There are not many methods that have been certified by the health department for disposing of human waste that does not include utilizing a conventional toilet in conjunction with a septic system or a composting toilet. In any event, having toilets and latrines available is necessary in order to guarantee the clean and sanitary disposal of human waste.

The following is a rundown of the fundamentals of primitive toilets and latrines:

- ➢ If it is at all feasible, you should install some kind of privacy barrier.
- ➢ Put toilets or latrines in a separate building from the places where food is prepared or eaten.

- Ensure that toilets and latrines are located at least 100 feet downstream from drinking water supplies and habitations, as well as at least 100 feet away from any bodies of surface water (rivers, lakes, reservoirs, etc.) and at least 100 feet away from any other bodies of water.
- If at all feasible, place a sink with running water, toilet paper, soap, paper towels, and trash disposal in close proximity to the bathroom's commode. If that is not an option, then hand sanitizer should be made accessible. In order to stop the spread of serious gastrointestinal infections, it is important to encourage people to regularly wash their hands and use hand sanitizer. When the toilet or latrine is not being used, the door or any coverings of any type should be kept covered to reduce the amount of stink and the number

of insects and animals that are attracted to the area.
- ➤ Think about utilizing portable toilets at the campsite.

Transient Toilets

This technique for disposing of human waste is well known among river guides and a small number of other outdoor enthusiasts. Even while the very idea of such a system makes us want to turn up our noses, it is, in reality, considerably easier to implement and much less complicated and dangerous than one would first believe.

Two sturdy plastic waste bags should be used to line the inside of a bucket with a capacity of 5 gallons or an old toilet bowl. Protect the valuables inside the bag by wrapping it up and stowing it out of the way so that no one will accidentally knock over the bucket as they try to avoid tripping over it.

When using the restroom, having a seat is really helpful. There is a plastic seat available at certain sports goods shops that may be used in buckets; however, these seats are somewhat weak. By epoxying a pair of guideposts to the bottom of a cheap toilet seat purchased from a hardware shop, the seat may be adapted to fit on the bucket in a secure and stable manner. When you've finished stuffing the bucket with waste bags to line it, you may attach the seat to the bucket.

To prevent the spread of disease and eliminate unpleasant odors, mix one cup of water with one cup of bleach containing three to six percent sodium hypochlorite once a day. Alternately, sprinkle some calcium oxide, often known as quicklime, over the excrement after each use. You may also use a liberal quantity (about half a cup) of cat litter, ashes, sawdust, or sand instead. If you just have a little bit of cat litter, you should first combine it with a filler (i.e., ashes, sand, or sawdust). There are several commercial chemicals that may be purchased at stores that provide sports goods and RV supplies; however, bleach, quicklime, or kitty litter can perform the job just as well at a fraction of the cost. These preventative measures suppress the development of bacteria and slow down the generation of methane gas. Paper towels and feminine hygiene items that have been used may be disposed of in the toilet.

It is recommended that a large trash bag be used to cover the toilet after each use in order to prevent flies from entering. Keep some hygiene supplies available. One bottle of hand sanitizer ought to be the very minimum need. An additional 5-gallon bucket filled with clean water and a bar of soap would be an even better option. Every day or two, you should switch out the water.

This arrangement is capable of satisfying the bathroom demands of two people for as long as a month, provided that there are no catastrophic bucket spills, but the splash factor will eventually become a serious worry at some time. At the completion of the process, put on some rubber gloves, remove any surplus air from the bags by squeezing them, and then tie the bags off to completely seal the box. Keep them in a place that is shielded from the elements, such as inside another bucket that has a cover, away from the direct sunlight, and in a location where animals and insects won't bother them, and the odor won't permeate living and eating spaces. After you have completed putting the toilet back together, you should wash your hands.

So, what exactly do you do with all of that garbage? You can't simply toss it in the trash or put it in the dumpster that's closest to you. It has to be transferred to a location that will not be unethical or unlawful, such as an authorized sanitary landfill, a dumping station, portable potty, camp outhouse, or any other location that meets those criteria. Do not just throw the bag in since the vast majority of these depositories are not designed to process garbage that is not sewage-related or composed of plastic. Put on some gloves made of disposable material and hold the bag over the opening. Make a cut in the corner of the bag using a pair of scissors that you have reserved just for that task. First, let as much as possible flow out, and then, using a tube of toothpaste as a model, squeeze the remaining substance out. Before placing the empty bag in the dumpster, place it inside an additional clean garbage bag and secure it with a knot. This will show consideration for the person who collects the trash. Clean both the scissors and your hands with soap and water.

Latrines

Simply said, a latrine is a pit that has been excavated to collect and store human excrement. Cat holes, which are small holes dug in the ground for single use, may range all the way up to the enormous pit and trench latrines designed for public use. Latrines are not suitable for urban locations that will continue to be used as areas for human habitation or commercial activity because it is difficult to determine the location of the hardpan or water table without first digging into the ground. The hygienic issues that have been carried over will be unpleasant.

Here are some of the fundamentals of the restroom:

- The depth of public latrines should be at least three feet, although they should be at least one foot above the hardpan or the water table.
- It is recommended that the "doodie" be covered with mud, lime, or ash after each usage in order to control the stench and reduce the risk of being infested by insects and other animals.

Off Grid Living

- When the latrine is not in use, you might think about covering it with an old piece of board.

Conclusion

I have been fortunate enough to go to several nations throughout the globe, and without fail, I have found that the people who reside in rural regions are the most hospitable and easiest to strike up a discussion with. It's possible that living off the grid will be a lot of fun. Take pleasure in the journey of being as self-reliant as you possibly can. The benefits are quite satisfying!

References:

1. *Cordwood Building: The State of the Art by Rob Roy (New Society Publishers, 2003).*

2. *Design Like You Give a Damn: Architectural Responses to Humanitarian Crises (Architecture for Humanity) by Kate Stohr, Cameron Sinclair (Metropolis Books, 2006).*

3. *Earthbag Building: The Tools, Tricks, and Techniques (Natural Building Series) by Kaki Hunter, Donald Kiffmeyer (New Society Publishers, 2004).*

4. *Earth-Sheltered Houses: How to Build an Affordable Underground Home by Rob Roy (New Society Publishers, 2006).*

5. *The Homeowner's Guide to Renewable Energy: Achieving Energy Independence through Solar, Wind, Biomass, and Hydropower by Dan Chiras (New Society Publishers, 2006).*

6. *The Art of Natural Building by Joseph F. Kennedy, Michael Smith, Catherine Wanek (New Society Publishers, 2002).*

7. *Building with Cob: A Step-by-Step Guide by Adam Weismann, Katy Bryce (Green Books, 2006).*

8. *Building with Earth: A Guide to Flexible-Form Earthbag Construction (A Real Goods Solar Living Book) by Paulina Wojciechowska (Chelsea Green, 2001).*

9. *The Cob Builders Handbook: You Can Hand-Sculpt Your Own Home by Becky Bee (Groundworks, 1998).*

10. *The Complete Yurt Handbook by Paul King (Eco-Logic Books, 2002).*

Printed in Great Britain
by Amazon